GLI

SATHER CLASSICAL LECTURES

Volume Thirty-four

SCENES FROM GREEK DRAMA

SCENES

FROM

GREEK DRAMA

BY BRUNO SNELL, *1896—*

UNIVERSITY OF CALIFORNIA PRESS

BERKELEY AND LOS ANGELES, 1967

University of California Press
Berkeley and Los Angeles, California

Cambridge University Press
London, England

© 1964 by The Regents of the University of California

Second printing, 1967

Library of Congress Catalog Card No.: 64-19110

Manufactured in the United States of America

PREFACE

WHEN, almost four years ago, I received the kind invitation from the Department of Classics at the University of California, Berkeley, to give the fiftieth Sather Lectures at this famous university, I felt honored yet embarrassed to be bracketed with so many distinguished scholars. I had just then decided not to take on any new obligations—those I had upon my shoulders already were a sufficient burden for the last years of my life. But then it occurred to me that I might combine these older duties with the lectures, and for this reason I chose the unattractive title: *Scenes from Greek Drama.* About thirty years ago I planned a new edition of the *Tragicorum Graecorum Fragmenta* by Nauck, and I have been working on that plan ever since with varying intensity, though other work has distracted me from this main task of my life. The collection of these fragments was accompanied by some thoughts about the reconstruction of lost Greek tragedies. So I thought I might present some reflections on one or two lost Greek plays on which I had been working for some time.

Alas, research has a curious tendency of going its own way besides or even against one's own intentions. When I settled down to look at Aeschylus' *Achilleis,* I had to treat a papyrus fragment, in fact, the longest piece of this trilogy we possess. But distinguished scholars have declared that it is spurious or at least doubtful. The strongest argument for its authenticity is, I believe, that a thought is expressed there (as it seems, for the first time) that is closely related to ideas put forward for the first time by Aeschylus in his preserved dramas. So I found myself sitting on my old hobby horse: tracing modern concepts to their first appearance in Greek poetry.

The same happened again when I tried my hand at Euripides' first *Hippolytos*. A discussion has long been going on whether Seneca's *Phaedra* can be used for the reconstruction of this lost tragedy. The last author, and a most eminent one, who has dwelled upon this subject is skeptical on this point. Here too, I think, it is possible to develop strong arguments from "Geistesgeschichte" to decide this question.

I know, it is widely believed that such arguments are vague. But I hope to show that it is possible to be exact in this interpretation and that one may gain results with it unattainable in other ways.

Of course, I had to apply the same method in treating the other plays I had chosen. It was not difficult to apply similar thoughts to them. I only hope one will not wonder with Horace why something that was meant to be an amphora turned out a common jug.

Though I shall necessarily have to be philological in the worst sense of the word—pedantic, quarreling about the exact meaning of Greek phrases and about the indiscreet question of who cribbed what from whom, I hope to present a bit of a thrilling experience: For me, at any rate, the rapid development of Greek thought in the fifth century B.C. is a fascinating spectacle, especially if one looks at the details that so often escape even close observation. And since these new ideas became a possession of Western civilization, we can observe ourselves growing.

The last two chapters will discuss a satyr play performed in the headquarters of Alexander the Great in India; besides they will themselves be a kind of satyr play, showing what farce can be made from what the Greeks in classical times had gained.

ACKNOWLEDGMENTS

I am indebted to the University of California for inviting me to deliver these Sather Lectures in October and November, 1963, and to my colleagues of the Classics Department in Berkeley for their many valuable suggestions. Above all, I am grateful to Professors Joseph Fontenrose and W. K. Pritchett who have made my visit in Berkeley one of the most pleasant experiences of my life.

I also owe thanks to the staff of the University of California Press, to Mr. Roy Curtis Giles (Eton), Mrs. M. Ross (Berkeley), and Mrs. M. Tubach (Berkeley) for their valuable help in preparing the English text of these lectures.

Berkeley, February, 1964   B. S.

CONTENTS

I

Shame and Guilt: Aeschylus' Achilles

For Plato, Achilles is a great hero (*Apol.* 28 D, *Symp.* 179 E) because he chooses to die young for the sake of immortal glory.[1] Ever since, we think of him in much the same way as Goethe, for example, describes him in his "Achilleis" (515):

> Alle Völker verehren
> Deine treffliche Wahl des kurzen rühmlichen Lebens,

"All nations venerate/ Thy seemly choice of the short and glorious life."

We are inclined to read this picture of Achilles into Homer as well, although he never mentions Achilles' choice. In the Iliad, it is true, we experience at first hand the slowly developing certainty that he will die young. We also hear that he is destined either to die a young and glorious death or to live a long and inglorious life, but nowhere does Homer mention Achilles' own conscious decision to make the nobler choice.

I should like to begin at a point where, in my view, we could first speak of a genuine decision on Achilles' part—that is, in Attic drama.

Achilles, the greatest of the Greeks in the Trojan war, is the

---

[1] This chapter has previously been read as the Philipp Maurice Deneke Lecture, 1963, at Lady Margaret Hall, Oxford. I wish to thank the governing body of Lady Margaret Hall, that they allowed me to defer the publication to this occasion.

central figure of only one ancient tragedy, it would seem, the Achilles trilogy of Aeschylus. We cannot prove—indeed, as we shall see, it is not even probable—that Aeschylus expressly mentioned Achilles' decision, but in the trilogy the figure of Achilles takes on a new dimension which for the first time makes a genuine decision possible, and he acquires over-all a new awareness of what he is doing.

Aeschylus' Achilles trilogy has not been preserved. We know something of it from quotations made by authors, from the Latin fragments of the *Myrmidons* and from *Achilles* of Accius which is obviously modeled faithfully on Aeschylus' play, and even more from papyrus fragments which have come to light during the past thirty years. The fragment edited by Norsa-Vitelli (fr. 225 Mette) is important, although the Professores Regii of Oxford and Cambridge, Lloyd-Jones and Page, doubt whether it belongs here. In it Achilles, annoyed that Agamemnon has taken Briseis away from him, withdraws from the battle against the Trojans with the result that the Trojans carry the day. Thereupon the Greeks send someone, apparently the son of Nestor, Antilochus, to Achilles and threaten him with stoning if he does not return to the battle. Aeschylus is the first to mention the stoning,[2] and as a futile attempt to force Achilles to rejoin the battle this scene roughly corresponds to the Homeric Presbeia.

The Iliad does not really explain the contradiction between Achilles' persistence in his anger and his decision to send out Patroclus. The action demands that he withdraw from the battle but also that the Greeks receive help:

There is some play made of the possibility of making Achilles be bound by an oracle (Π 36 f.), but the possibility is not expressly exploited. Much more does Achilles characterize his own behavior as inner inconsistency and indecision (Π 60 f.). Later (Σ 450) Thetis reporting the matter in short before Hephaestus mentions that Achilles sent Patroclus into the battle (cf. Wilamowitz, *Ilias und Homer*, p. 173). Here, therefore, Aeschylus was obliged to invent

---

[2] Euripides later takes up the theme, *Iph. A.* 1349 f.

another motivation if he was to make Patroclus' entry into battle the central point of the first play in his Achilles trilogy.[3]

The stoning serves the purpose of making it psychologically impossible for Achilles to rejoin battle, for, obviously, Achilles cannot submit to such pressure. He merely becomes all the more obdurate.

In the papyrus the following conversation develops between Achilles and his interlocutor (Antilochus, we presume):[4]

ACHILLES: [What is the good] of their stoning my body? You needn't think that the son of Peleus, when his body is mutilated by stones, will ever desist in favor of the Trojans from the battle—from the weaponless battle—on the Trojan field.

ANTILOCHUS (?):   And yet that can happen. There you could find that easier way to what you call man's physician of suffering [death].

ACHILLES: Am I then to take up arms again for fear of the Achaeans—arms which I [had just put down] in anger at the bad leadership? [Well then!] If, as my confederates assert, I alone am the cause of such a devastating defeat, then I will [spoil] everything for the Achaean army. I am not ashamed to say such a thing. For who can maintain that such leaders and such military detachments are nobler than I?

If Aeschylus, in the first instance, only needed a motivation for Achilles' refusal to join battle, the motivation he chose was such that both opposing parties undergo a fundamental change, and that for both sides motives are put into play that were not there for Homer but which were of the highest significance for Aeschylus and his age.[5]

[3] C. E. Fritsch, "Neue Fragmente des Aischylos und Sophokles" doctoral dissertation, Hamburg, 1936, 24.

[4] For text see Appendix p. 139.

[5] The most thorough treatment of our fragment is W. Schadewaldt, *Hellas und Hesperien*, pp. 166-210 (= *Hermes*, 71, 1936, 25-69); for the difference between Homer and Aeschylus, see pp. 194-202.

With Homer, in the Presbeia (*Iliad*, book 9) it is Achilles' honor and reputation that are in question, and the envoys try in various ways to make Achilles realize that he will not lose face if he returns to the battle under the conditions which Agamemnon is now offering him—indeed that he will in the event win even greater honor (302 ff., 603 ff.). In Aeschylus' trilogy something different is at stake. When the Greeks threaten Achilles with stoning, they are claiming for themselves a right: the right to punish him. In the Iliad the legation can attempt to persuade Achilles, can offer him gifts so that he desists from his anger, can convince him (245) that he himself will be in difficulties if the Greeks are defeated, and can ask him, even if he is angry with Agamemnon, to have pity on the other Greeks (301); but they claim no pretext for taking legal proceedings against him, indeed they do not even appeal to something like comradeship.[6] The stoning[7] is a death penalty in which every member of the community has the right to take part. The punishment debars the criminal from society; it is a more severe form of outlawing. The man condemned to stoning is at liberty to flee but may be killed when in flight.

Death by stoning is by no means lynch justice; it follows βουλῇ δημοσίῃ, as Hipponax (77 Diehl) says, and is inflicted for sacramental crimes such as the desecration of temples. But

---

[6] Homer's nearest approach to what we should call comradeship is what Thetis (*Il.* 18, 128) says to Achilles when the latter after the death of Patroclus decides to join the battle after all: οὐ κακόν ἐστιν τειρομένοις ἑτάροισιν ἀμυνέμεν αἰπὺν ὄλεθρον. Achilles is determined to make Hector pay for Patroclus' death and thereby hopes to win renown. Thetis says: "It is no bad thing to defend one's distressed comrades against death," that is, "no one can blame you for helping your friends." As in other, similar instances in Homer, a good thing appears here negatively as a not-bad thing: there is nothing to be said against doing what is conventionally expected and need not be called "merit." Above all, it is not the willingness to help others as such that is here raised to a moral obligation, but the objective task "of defending each other against death"—much in the same way as Achilles ironically says elsewhere (Il. 9, 323) that just as a bird brings food for its unfledged young, so he had worked and fought hard day and night even when the only purpose of the war had been to provide Agamemnon with concubines.

[7] Rud. Hirzel, "Die Strafe der Steinigung," *Abh. Ak. Leipzig*, 1909, 225 ff. K. Latte, *RE.* see under "Steinigung." Schadewaldt *op. cit.*, pp. 171 f.

death by stoning is above all the punishment for deserters.
Here, too, it is originally part of sacramental law, for prayer
and sacrifice are offered before war and battle not only to
entreat for victory but also to strengthen the solidarity of the
warriors by an act of worship; he who forsakes a community
which is so constituted is subject to sacramental punishment.
We find stoning in Homer also but, needless to say, in a different
context. The following quotations will show in how different a
light Homer and Aeschylus saw stoning:

Hector to Paris in *Iliad* (3, 56):

> ἀλλὰ μάλα Τρῶες δειδήμονες· ἦ τέ κεν ἤδη
> λάϊον ἔσσο χιτῶνα κακῶν ἔνεχ' ὅσσα ἔοργας.

Eteocles in Aeschylus' *Seven against Thebes* (196 ff.):

> κεἰ μή τις ἀρχῆς τῆς ἐμῆς ἀκούσεται
> ἀνὴρ γυνή τε χὤτε τῶν μεταίχμιον,
> ψῆφος κατ' αὐτῶν ὀλεθρία βουλεύσεται,
> λευστῆρα δήμου δ' οὔτι μὴ φύγῃ μόρον.

Eteocles sees himself as the responsible commander in the field
bringing to lawful punishment the man who does not obey
orders. Hector, on the other hand, is of the opinion that Paris,
because the war with the Greeks and the ensuing danger for
the city were the direct results of the rape of Helen, had placed
himself outside society and deserved to be stoned. But the
common action breaks down, "the Trojans are too cowardly,
or else they would bury[8] you under stones for what you have
done."

Homer and Aeschylus differ from each other considerably
both in the facts and in the judicial proceedings. There is no
doubt that Paris had committed a crime; there is no doubt that
he had endangered the safety of the city in such a way that the
state would have to intervene. But such a state with an effective

---

[8] For the phrase "to put on the stone shirt," cf. Alk. 24 A 17 D. = 129 L.-P.
ἀλλ' ἢ θάνοντες γᾶν ἐπιέμμενοι κείσεσθ' ὑπ' ἀνδρῶν ... Sim. 67, 4 on the snow which
one "buries" so that it may remain alive: ζωὴ Πιερίην γῆν ἐπιεσσαμένη. Further:
E. Fraenkel's commentary on Aesch. *Ag.* 872.

legal system obviously does not exist. Hector says the Trojans are δειδήμονες, timid. The community fails to execute its right to punish obviously because no one is willing to proceed against a prince.

Eteocles, on the other hand, threatens with stoning not in the event of a crime being committed or damage being done to the state, but simply in the event of insubordination. This presupposes that Eteocles is speaking on behalf of a state which must be obeyed. Such a conception of the state is a post-Homeric development; it was naturally asserted above all in time of war, which is what Eteocles is doing.

This is also the case in Aeschylus' Achilles trilogy. Some-body—we cannot tell who it is, Agamemnon perhaps, or the council of kings—claims to make demands on the individual and to punish any insubordination that may occur. We are not told whether staying away from the battle was considered de-sertion, but it is definitely called "treason," which is punishable by stoning.[9] The chorus of Myrmidons, that is, Achilles' own followers, reproach him with treason. At least one ancient lexicographer[10] maintains that "at the beginning of the play," in the anapaests with which it makes its entrance, the chorus of Myrmidons had used the word προπίνειν in speaking to Achilles meaning "to commit treason".[11] In a further frag-ment,[12] that may have followed more or less on the first, we read—and the words are evidently directed at Achilles: "lest you betray the Hellenic army," and in the dialogue with

,

---

[9] E.g., Aristoph. *Ach.* 281 βάλλε τὸν προδότην (sc. Dikaiopolis). Further Schadewaldt p. 172.

[10] Fr. 212A M.

[11] *Schol. Pind.*, o. 7,5 (I, 200, 11 Dr.) προπίνειν ἐστὶ κυρίως τὸ ἅμα τῷ κράματι τὸ ἀγ-γεῖον χαρίζεσθαι. It is quite possible that it is symposium jargon to say προπίνειν for προδιδόναι. Cf. Anacreon fr. 407 P. and Demosth. 18, 296. In any case, the lexicographer who quoted this use of προπίνειν for Aeschylus must have known that Achilles was accused of treason.

[12] Fr. 221 M. We can add to this Accius' *Achilles* fr. 1: *qua re alia ex crimine inimicorm effugere possis, delica*, "explain how else you can escape the accusation of your enemies." As long ago as 1873 Ribbeck had concluded that Achilles was accused of treason. His view holds good.

Antilochus (?) Achilles says (20): "he has reproached me with treason," προδοσίαν ἔνειμ᾽ ἐμοί.[13] As apparently no other ancient writer calls Achilles' refusal to join battle treason, this passage strongly supports the view that the fragment really belongs to the *Myrmidons*.

I shall not examine here how far this legal interpretation that mere insubordination constitutes treason, and that such treason deserves death by stoning, is in accordance with the legal conditions as they existed in early times or in Aeschylus' own day. If Aeschylus used old motives here, he did so in order to make both portrayable and plausible something thoroughly modern, namely the state's insistence that an objectively valid, strict order be kept—the state's right to enforce civic duties.

Exactly how Achilles meets the state's claim to obedience is not clear. From what *is* discernible he neither questions the right fundamentally nor recognizes it absolutely—either course would estrange him too much from the Homeric Achilles, who knows nothing of such rights. And so Aeschylus, in his wisdom, apparently refrains from making him discuss it at all.

On the other hand, by comparison with Homer, he intensifies the claim that portrays Achilles as the ablest of the Greeks. He calls himself εὐγενέστερος (13), more noble, than the rest of the princes, which he is beyond doubt as he alone has a goddess for a mother. But Homer's Achilles does not boast in this manner of the greater honor that is his due.[14]

Again by comparison with Homer's Achilles, Aeschylus' hero emphasizes his qualities as a warrior differently, so much so that he would seem to balance himself off against the other princes and the Greeks who claim to represent the community.[15]

But all these Homeric motives of honor and rancor, pride and outrage, would not be enough, even in this intensification, to outbalance the absolute claim of law which the Greeks raise against him.

---

[13] For text, see below, p. 139.

[14] See Schadewaldt, p. 177.

[15] It is doubtful whether Achilles was alluding here to his bravery against Kyknos; see below, Appendix p. 142.

One sentence, above all others, characterizes Aeschylus' Achilles (12): "shame does not keep me back from uttering such a word," τοῖον] δ' ἀφεῖναι τοῦπος οὐκ αἰδώς μ'ἔχει. This almost certainly refers to the fact that he is prepared to destroy the whole Greek army.[16] He knows that by saying this openly he is disregarding the αἰδώς, the shame, but in his indignation he considers his action justified.[17] The first man in Greece to offend against the αἰδώς and the social convention and to boast about it was Archilochus who lost his shield on the field of battle— a great disgrace. But the difference between Archilochus and Aeschylus' Achilles is great: Archilochus, in an emergency, has done something which the others consider to be ignominious; he, however, shows that it was expedient and the right thing to do, thereby saving his life.[18] Aeschylus' Achilles, however, throws shame and decency overboard in pursuit of an aim of his own which he considers right; it is the others who are intent on injustice. When one of the old poets breaks through conventional opinions, he unmasks something that is acknowledged as foolish or immaterial. Judgment on conventional action is therefore scorn and contempt. Achilles' contradiction goes deeper: in the sharply contrasted either–or of right and wrong, it is a matter of principles which brook no rival. "I am not ashamed" means: I do not care what you think. I shall stand by what I have done, by my convictions, and shall carry it through against your resistance.

Another marked contrast with what Achilles says are the words somebody uses in Sappho (fr. 137 L.–P.)—Alcaeus according to Aristotle—"I am going to say something, but shame prevents me" (θέλω τί τ'εἴπην, ἀλλά με κωλύει αἰδως), a sign that the words had no noble or beautiful purpose. Here, too,

---

[16] See Appendix p. 142. The other possibility would be for Achilles to say: "I am not ashamed to say that I alone am worth all the Greek princes put together."

[17] Even in the case that this should be pure *hubris* (i.e., with no consciousness of right), as we find it for instance in words of Clytemnestra to be discussed soon, it must be acknowledged that this kind of *hubris* too cannot exist before one can claim a personal right.

[18] Fr. 6 D. The correct text no doubt is: ἐξέφυγον θανάτου τέλος.

shame is violated: he who says that shame prevents him from speaking is already confessing his love but at the same time acknowledging the αἰδώς. This elegant game, this modest attempt to break through the convention, has nothing of the challenging conceit of Achilles.

True it is, however, that the sentence beginning "I am not ashamed" has the same Achillean tone in other places in Aeschylus' works, however different may be the people who speak it and however different the situations in which they do so. Aeschylus is the first to give it this tone, as far as I know, and when it appears several times in his work, this proves that it had a special significance for him and demonstrates once again that the conversation between Achilles and Antilochus was written by him. When Clytemnestra hears that Troy has fallen and that Agamemnon is on his way home, she tells the herald (*Ag.* 587 ff.) to report to her husband that she has kept house faithfully, has taken delight in no other man (which is, of course, a lie), and preserved her reputation. "And so I pride myself in my truthfulness, and such boastful pride is no disgrace for a noblewoman" (613 f.: οὐκ αἰσχρὸς ὡς γυναικὶ γενναίᾳ λακεῖν). What she means is that shame forbids such boastfulness—and precisely in such matters—but as a noblewoman and because it is the truth, I am infringing the αἰδώς.[19] This is a trick to entice Agamemnon into her trap, but nevertheless she can reproach Agamemnon for several things that really weigh heavily to his disadvantage. I shall return to this point in my next chapter when I shall discuss the guilt of Phaedra in Euripides' *Hippolytos*. It appears that for Aeschylus a self-confident person can speak like this, against convention, in the name of truth.

Clytemnestra speaks like this on more than one occasion. On Agamemnon's entrance she says to the chorus (855): "Citizens . . . I shall not be ashamed to speak of my love for my husband [οὐκ αἰσχυνοῦμαι]"; once again she is pretending. But in the deadliest earnest she says after she has murdered

---

[19] Cf. Denniston-Page on this point.

Agamemnon, "I do not feel shame to speak the opposite of all that I said before to suit the situation [οὐκ ἐπαισχυνθήσομαι] for how else could I reach my goal . . . Now I have attained what I wanted and I shall not disclaim this [1380: καὶ τάδ' οὐκ ἀρνήσομαι]." She acknowledges having committed the deed although she knows what a deed it was. Whereas Achilles leaves shame aside in order to say something he believes himself genuinely justified in saying, Clytemnestra shouts her crime from the roof tops, though later she says to the chorus (1497): "*Thou* art confident that this deed is mine . . . but appearing in the shape of this dead man's wife, the ancient fierce spirit that takes vengeance for the misdeed of the cruel feaster Atreus has now rendered this full-grown man as payment to the young, a crowning sacrifice" (translated by Ed. Fraenkel). Herewith Clytemnestra returns to the old mythical motivation of man's actions:[20] that is to say, her self-confidence collapses. What she had pretended to be her right turns out to have been *hubris*, and a dual aspect of the new concept of man's own actions becomes apparent: This new idea of justice and *dike* can be misused and may deliver a person all the more cruelly to the Ate, the Alastor, and the daemons. But, nevertheless, Achilles and Clytemnestra have in common—and Aeschylus was the first to say it—that a man, by rejecting shame, stands up for what he does and says as for his own dearest possession.

There are many passages in Homer where a hero boasts of his own deeds, and in fact this boasting (εὔχεσθαι) is typical of a warrior who has slain his adversary. Often it borders on *hubris*. But the difference cannot be overlooked: the Homeric εὔχεσθαι means to proclaim loudly, solemnly, so to speak with swollen breast, and according to the situation it may be praying, vowing, or boasting. It may be vain bragging, but then the moral fault is simply that the boasting exceeds the allowed measure. The quantity of it makes *hubris*. A Homeric hero boasts on a certain occasion when a god has given him κῦδος, that is, a

---

[20] Cf. A. Lesky, *S B Heid., phil.-hist. Kl.* 1961, 4, p. 52.

superiority and elevation. There it is his right and almost his duty to proclaim his deed so that he may be duly recognized, whereas Achilles and Clytemnestra scoff at what others may say about them.

The Prometheus of Aeschylus makes the same assertion as Clytemnestra in the passage just quoted when he assumes responsibility for stealing fire for the benefit of man (266): "It was of my own free will that I did wrong, I shall not deny it," ἑκὼν ἑκὼν ἥμαρτον, οὐκ ἀρνήσομαι. But it is with pride that he says that he has done wrong although shame ought to forbid him to say such a thing.[21]

Prometheus' deed, which he admits, can be defended morally, though it is not free from *hubris*. Clytemnestra's cannot be defended. Achilles' deed is problematical, and we shall see to what extent. But every one of these persons—and this is something new—evokes us to ask and to reflect upon what is right, what is wrong, what is responsibility, what is *hubris*. The account is no longer settled as easily as before. For Aeschylus, the idea that the law must hold good absolutely and without limit has two sides to it: on the one, the state demands the unconditional observance of its legal system; on the other, man develops an awareness that whenever right is on his side, he must stand up for it unconditionally.

The sentence, "I am not ashamed to do or say what I consider to be right" expresses with particular pregnancy the contrast between a primitive shame culture and a more sophisticated guilt culture, which ethnologists in the United States have worked out and which E. R. Dodds in his Sather Lectures has applied to classical Greece,[22] for the sentence means: "I surrender my reputation and rely on what is right, my right."

---

[21] Cf. *Philol. Suppl.*, 20, 1, pp. 97 f. With less pride Orestes (*Eum.* 588) says: τούτου δ'οὔτις ἄρνησις πέλει and (611): δρᾶσαι γάρ, ὥσπερ ἔστιν, οὐκ ἀρνήσομαι, but still with the same awareness that it is a matter of his own deed.

[22] E. R. Dodds, *The Greeks and the Irrational*, Berkeley and Los Angeles, 1951, especially chap. 2, Dodds (p. 26, n. 106) quotes Ruth Benedict, *The Chrysanthemum and the Sword*, who (especially on pp. 222 ff.) uses this distinction to work out the difference between Japanese and Puritan American morality.

This means, however, that what had been valid as a standard before the fifth century is no longer so for the men that Aeschylus portrays. Shame culture, at least in Greece, implies a strict order of values in society and of acknowledged religious ties, that leave no genuine freedom of decision. The awareness of what is right increases gradually, and the preliminary stages of what we learn from Aeschylus have been there since Hesiod. I shall not go into this now but should like briefly to touch on two points relevant to Aeschylus' Achilles.

Archilochus, in the Strassburg Epode (fr. 79 D.), curses someone who, though bound in friendship to him by oath, has betrayed him; he ends the poem with these words: "Who has done wrong to me and has trodden on the oaths with his feet, though once he was my friend," ὅs μ' ἠδίκησε, λὰξ δ' ἐπ' ὁρκί-οισ' ἔβη τὸ πρὶν ἑταῖρος ἐών. Archilochus here reacts to the wrong he has suffered no less passionately than Aeschylus' Achilles, but there is a difference. Achilles seeks to set the wrong he has suffered to rights by doing something himself, not only by rebuke, nor even, as Hesiod does, by exhortation (*paraenesis*); he believes himself justified and obliged to see his own right through by doing something about it.

Archilochus had already taken a step from shame culture to guilt culture[23] by saying that the right had been violated, ὅs μ' ἠδίκησε, whereas in Homer Achilles, who complains to his mother Thetis of how Agamemnon has treated him, speaks of offended honor (*Il.* 1, 355: ἦ γάρ μ' 'Ατρεΐδης . . . ἠτίμησεν). Archilochus, and Alcaeus alike shortly afterward, sees in the perjury of their friend rather a violation of a personal trust, and for them it is not altogether a question of the conflict of two antagonistic legal claims.

Solon's contribution to this development is also substantial. In the works of the Athenian poet both the absolute value of the objective legal order and the unrestricted sway of the personal awareness of what is right as foundations of the state

---

[23] This has already been pointed out: H. Gundert, *Das neue Bild der Antike*, I, 137, n. 2.

are seen more clearly than anywhere else before Aeschylus.[24] But Solon's unflinching belief in Zeus as the guarantor of the law removes any suggestion of conflict. Thus he can still unabashedly ask the gods to grant him wealth and reputation and to let him live to the benefit of his friends and to the detriment of his enemies[25] (1, 1 ff.): "I yearn for wealth but should not like to come by it by unrightful means."

These archaic notions that a man can win merit in the esteem of his fellows and that he can assert himself by helping his friends and injuring his enemies were shown by Aeschylus to be shallow although, of course, they have survived him. Out of the new tension between the legal claim of the state and the individual's awareness of what is right arises the irreconcilability which Sophocles later portrayed between Antigone and Creon. The Homeric heroes are far more capable of deliberating over the claim to honor and the granting of it; for there it is a question of the "due portion," and one can try to come to a settlement by persuasion. Where there are rival legal claims, one must try to convince the other with cogent arguments.

In Aeschylus' *Achilleis* the hero's claim to assert his own self far surpasses the legal sphere. The greatness and the danger of this new self-assertiveness is revealed in the way in which Achilles, later in the play, after Patroclus has gone into battle and fallen, expresses his grief for his friend.[26] Homer describes (*Il.* 18, 22 ff.) the mourning Achilles in his gestures and chiefly, however much he may reach the heights of a magnificent pathos, in the ritual lamentation ceremonies: Achilles covers his head with dust, throws himself to the ground, and tears his hair. Homer further portrays the cries of the slave girls who beat their breasts and fall faint, and describes how Antilochus weeps and holds Achilles' hand for fear he might cut his throat (with the iron). As far as the "psychical" aspect

---

[24] Cf. *Poetry and Society*, pp. 38 ff.

[25] Cf. A. Dihle, *Die goldene Regel*, pp. 32 f.

[26] Schadewaldt (pp. 198 ff.) has dealt with this correctly and impressively. I am not repeating it but merely trying to fill in some details.

is concerned, we are merely told (but not in the words of the victims themselves) that Achilles is enshrouded in a black cloud of grief, that the slave girls are full of sorrow in their *thymos* (ἀκαχημένοι), that Achilles laments his friend (ὀδύρετο), and that he sighs in his heart (ἔστενε κυδάλιμον κῆρ) and sobs frightfully (σμερδαλέον δ' ᾤμωξε).

Homer raises the lament to a superhuman level in the scene that follows (35 f.): news of what has happened reaches Achilles' mother, the immortal Thetis, on the sea bed where she is sitting next to her aged father Nereus. There she lets out a cry of woe, and all the goddesses of the depths, the Nereids, gather around her. There follows the so-called Nereid catalogue, a long succession of their resounding names, and we are told that they all strike their breasts simultaneously.[27] The customary lamentation of the women which was first begun by the slave girls and familiar to us, for example, in the Dipylon vases, is then taken up by the gods, which increases the stature, portent, and sublimity of the lamentation. But that is not all. The names of the Nereids: Glauce, Nesaea, Galateia, Actaea, Cymodoce, Cymothoe, paint for us a charming picture of the sea as it spreads out before our eyes,[28] and with it the lamentation is clarified; now Thetis can speak in calmer words of her present grief and of the grief which awaits her.

What a different picture it is that Aeschylus gives us! The few words from Achilles' lament for his slaughtered friend that have survived are penetrated through and through with personal, intense passion. Even here Achilles speaks with a complete awareness that what had been his is so genuine and significant that he can disregard convention and shame. Aeschylus conceives the friendship between Achilles and Patroclus as an erotic relationship. True, he found such a tie less repugnant than would generally be true today, but the ruthless way in which Achilles speaks about it goes further

---

[27] On the meaning of the Nereid catalogue in this connection, see Schadewaldt, *Von Homers Welt und Werk*, 1944, 249.

[28] *Entd. d. Geistes³*, 1955, 68 f.

than what we usually hear. It must have shocked even the Athenians when Achilles looks on the friendship as something sacred and speaks of the "chaste consecration of the thighs" and the "devout union of the thighs":

σέβας δὲ μηρῶν ἁγνὸν οὐκ ἐπῃδέσω
ὦ δυσχάριστε τῶν πυκνῶν φιλημάτων (fr. 228 M.),

ἡ ξυναυ]λία δ' ἐκ[εῖ
μηρῶν τε τῶν σῶν εὐσεβὴς ὁμιλία (fr. 229 M.).

When, in the first sentence, he reproaches Patroclus for infringing the αἰδώς, the respect for the pious bond, and his ingratitude for the many kisses, it is clear that the relation between them is more personal than when Archilochus or Alcaeus complained of a breach of oath as a friend has become a foe. With Aeschylus it is a question of personal happiness in tender companionship, an attachment that has grown beyond the earlier notion of friendship with friends living for the benefit of each other but to the detriment of their enemies. And it points in advance to questions to be raised later by Euripides in *Alcestis, Medea,* and *Phaedra*.

Above all, the Aeschylean Achilles shows his readiness to stand by his own word and deed by being to blame, as he himself says, for Patroclus' death having given him his own armor and sent him into the battle. Homer's Achilles knew too that he had sent Patroclus to his death, but he knew it only in the uncommitting way in which all Homer's figures know of their guilt—without genuine responsibility, without being fully convinced that they themselves have *really* done something. A comparison with Homer makes this clear.

In book 18 of the Iliad Achilles says to Thetis (79 ff.): "My one wish [that the Greeks be beaten back] Zeus has granted; but what pleasure have I in it? For my dear companion, whom I honored above all others, and in like measure as my own person, is dead. It was I who sent him to his destruction [ἀπώλεσα], while Hector is in possession of his armor . . . Now my *thymos* calls upon me not to live and be one of the people unless Hector has paid for it with his life." Homer's Achilles says, "It was I who sent him to his destruction," not, however, with a full consciousness of being himself at fault, but in resignation, for when he goes on to reflect how it all came about he curses the anger (χόλος) which makes even a reasonable man lose his temper—"in the same manner as Agamemnon had made me angry. But let bygones be bygones for all our sorrows, curbing perforce the *thymos* in our breasts" (111–113). Even if Achilles does not say, more or less like Agamemnon (19, 86 ff.), "Zeus, fate, and the fury are more to blame than I",[29] as far as Achilles is concerned and in spite of his avowal: "It was I who sent him to his destruction," it is not really he who is to blame, but a passing emotional disturbance.

Aeschylus' Achilles, who has thrown all consideration for the opinion of others to the winds, who has taken on himself the responsibility for everything that has happened, could no longer speak like this after everything had turned out badly. He knows that it was he who was responsible for his friend's death and knows that it is he who is affected most deeply by it. "Antilochus, weep rather for me than for him who is dead. Weep for me who am alive, for I have lost my all" (fr. 227 M.). He quotes the fable of the eagle struck by a plumed arrow and says, "It is not by some alien agency, nay, but by our own plumes that we are struck down" (fr. 231 M.). If Achilles realizes that he is to blame for Patroclus' death, life is made even more bitter for him than it had been in the previous scene where he had spoken of "death as the physician of suffering" (fr. 225, 6 M.). At all events, he must now have gone into his last battle in full knowledge of his early death and with the will to die.[30]

---

[29] For this form of self-reflection, see the excellent analysis by Dodds, *The Greeks and the Irrational*, pp. 3 ff.

[30] The wish to die has here a quite different sound than when Sappho, for example, says τεθνάκην ἀδόλως θέλω (fr. 94, 1 L.-P.) or when elsewhere in earlier poetry the thought is expressed that it is better to die than to live: for Aeschylus here it is the *moral* existence and therewith the essence of a self-assertive human being that is destroyed. Needless to say, other versions of this motive occur in Aeschylus, for example in the words attributed to Priam (fr. 249 M.); cf. Pearson's commentary on Soph. fr. 698.

Now there is scarcely any room for a choice between a long, inglorious life and an early, glorious death—indeed, such a choice would look rather pitiful, not to say philistine, when we think of the Achilles we have met elsewhere in the fragments of Aeschylus' *Achilleis*. Nor does it fit into our image of the shame culture (that is why it is not found in Homer,[31] for there no conflict of values exists, which is a later idea) or, as it happens, into the guilt culture, for there, it is not the glory (κλέος) that plays the decisive role, but the right, and indeed the right is the important thing in all that is extant of Aeschylus' works. Of course, it is not certain that Aeschylus was unable to give this motif of choice and vital decision a significant twist of his own. Perhaps Achilles did go to his death after all with a proud "albeit" on his lips like Eteocles, for instance (who does not merely push aside the thought of glory and reputation either—see lines 7 and 683 ff.—although there something else is at stake), thereby sublimating the thought of glory both morally and legally beyond the Homeric conception. That would mean, of course, a mixture of motives which, strictly speaking, are not compatible. Friedrich Mehmel has shown[32] that the Achilles of Plato's *Apologia* (28 D) has such a disunity. Socrates quotes there book 18 of the Iliad, where Thetis says to Achilles that he would die soon after avenging the death of Patroclus (96). Plato's Achilles answers, "So be it then." Homer's Achilles begins with these words as well (98), but Socrates paraphrases further, "lest I remain a laughingstock." Mehmel says correctly that there is a fundamental difference between Homer's Achilles and Socrates who appeals to himself for his readiness to die. The difference is

---

[31] Cf. R. Pfeiffer, *DLZ.*, 56, 1935, 2131 ff. in his article on W. Jaeger's *Paideia*, Vol. I, unfortunately not included in his selected writings (but cf. here, p. 44, n. 2) and E. R. Schwinge, *Hypomnemata*, 1, 1962, 103 ff. (with Schadewaldt's expositions quoted there). I do not intend to go into the copious literature here which deals with the problem of decision and with the history of the discovery of the Ego; it is quoted by K. Oehler, *Die Lehre vom noetischen und dianoetischen Denken bei Platon und Aristoteles in Zetemata*, 29, 1962, 4 f. (Oehler, p. 3., deals especially with the importance of the consciousness of guilt for this development.)

[32] *Antike und Abendland*, 4, 1954, 28.

that Homer's Achilles by his death wins the acknowledgment
and respect of the community in which he lives, by doing what
is expected of a nobleman according to the code of the time.
Socrates, on the other hand, does precisely the opposite; he
takes his stand against the community with which he is in-
compatible and accepts death. Indeed, for Homer's hero, it is
important not to become a laughingstock. But for Socrates that
is no matter of his own concern. And so Socrates interpolates
four words between the two sentences we have quoted, which
Homer's Achilles does not say: δίκην ἐπιθεὶς τῷ ἀδικοῦντι,
"inflicting on him who has done wrong the right [i.e., the just]
punishment." Apparently without noticing it Socrates (or
Plato) imputes this idea of justice to the Homeric Achilles
which in reality is alien to him. Socrates had already said that
for a decent man faced with the choice between life and death
the main thing could only be "whether he is doing right or
wrong," πότερον δίκαια ἢ ἄδικα πράττει (28 B)—which proves
that he was concerned with something other than the "glorious
life."[33]

The motif of the stoning had already shown that Aeschylus
had introduced this concept of right, which was lacking in
Homer, at the point where Achilles stayed away from the
battle, as the unconditional claim of the community whether
as state or military power and at the same time as the irrevoc-
able legal claim of the individual. It is here that Aeschylus
departs essentially from Homer.

It may well be that Aeschylus, at a later stage in the trilogy,
portrayed what Plato, elsewhere, when he mentions once again
Achilles' conversation with his mother Thetis, puts this way:
he found himself able to choose (ἐτόλμησε ἑλέσθαι) death for
his lover Patroclus by bringing him help and avenging him
(Symp. 179 E); but if he did so, he had to deepen the motif of
glory to the effect that the real and genuine glory is that which

---

[33] Isocrates (Euag. 3) speaks without any difficulties about those ἀντὶ τοῦ ζῆν
ἀποθνῆσκειν εὐκόλως αἱρουμένους, καὶ μᾶλλον περὶ τῆς δόξης ἢ τοῦ βίου σπουδάζοντας, καὶ πάντα
ποιοῦντας ὅπως ἀθάνατον τὴν περὶ αὐτῶν μνήμην καταλείψουσιν.

man wins by standing up for what is right without thought for the opinion of the majority—and the voluntarily assumed atonement could also be what is right. Thus Plato does not say that Achilles won fame among men, but: "The gods admired him and honored him more than anybody else." These gods reward what is right. In the *Apologia* Socrates similarly sublimates the notion of divinity when he says he acts as he does "because the god so charges him to do so" (e.g., 28 E). No longer is that a divinity that gives (as was the general belief) helpful bits of advice now and then as in Homer, but a divinity that stands up for what is right, as a higher principle. And so glory, for Aeschylus, must be not the recognition won for a single heroic deed but the appreciation, by the judicious, of a rightful action.

But in order to establish the difference between Homer and the Platonic interpretation of his Achilles even more clearly, let us return once more to the Homeric dialogue between Thetis and Achilles and look closer still at two passages. Since we have learned from Aeschylus what a genuine deed and a genuine decision are, we can now understand better what Homer actually means, and why he does not speak of "deed" and "decision."[34] He says less, but on the other hand much more.

Achilles' words (90 ff.) are: "Not even [οὐδέ] my *thymos* commands me to live, unless I have first slain Hector and revenged the death of Patroclus." His temper, his passion, his joy (all this may lie in *thymos*—but certainly not his decision) tells him to wreak revenge on Hector though one should expect that the *thymos* would above all warn him of danger.

---

[34] As modern authors usually think he does, without being aware of their Platonic interpretation. I mention as one of the finest interpretations of the Homeric Achilles that of A. W. Gomme in his Sather Lectures *The Greek Attitude to Poetry and History* (p. 47). Gomme here aims at something very important and often overlooked, but in order to bring it forth we need not refer to "deed" and "decision" as he does. On the other hand, Gomme (p. 109) rightly points out that "free will is clearly implied" in the words of Kandaules' wife to Gyges (Herodot I, 11, 2): νῦν τοι δυοῖν ὁδῶν παρεουσέων, Γύγη, δίδωμι αἵρεσιν ὁκοτέρην βούλεαι τραπέσθαι. But I cannot follow him when he continues: "There is, in fact, no possible story ('poetic' story) about human beings which does not imply free will."

And then, line 114 ff.: "Now I shall go to slay Hector. Then I shall take up death if the gods want it. Even Heracles had to die: Moira and the wrath of Hera subdued him. So I too shall die if the same fate is prepared for me. But now I want to win glory by slaying Hector." Achilles does not make a choice between long life and glory but says in resignation: if I have to die I shall bear it, but at least I want to win glory before my death.

In the first passage he is driven forward by the stronger emotion, that is, his wish to revenge himself is stronger than the concern for his life. In the second passage he accepts death as inevitable—but certainly, he does not choose it. Homer's Achilles is the greatest hero among Greeks and Trojans, and at the same time he has deep insight into the frailty of man. He is a devoted friend, an attentive son, noble toward his equals even if they come on an unpleasant legation, and humane toward the father of his most bitter enemy. His acute sense of honor may raise in him a violent temper that enables him to accomplish great deeds, but that can plunge him into wrath and revenge. He can even be cruel, and yet he is not ashamed of his tears.

This Achilles is, so to speak, a great piece of human nature, great in all its aspects of vital and noble reactions, and what happens to him is greater than any personal decision.

For our modern viewpoint it may be difficult to see the difference between Homer and Aeschylus, because we cannot easily ignore what we have learned from Aeschylus and Plato. To me this difference seems to be fundamental.

I am not raising the question of whether Homer communicates a deeper truth about man than Aeschylus. I could imagine that someone might undertake to prove this. One may contend that the Greeks by bringing forth a special and perhaps limited knowledge about the working of the human mind had to give up something that we shall always admire in Homer. But when can man achieve something without paying for it dearly? The way of our civilization is the way which the Greeks took after

Homer, and I for my part do not hesitate to call this real progress and a new and higher concept of man.

But I do not want to become lost in speculations. So much at least is certain: that Aeschylus' Achilles is the first to become a man from whom one can expect genuine decisions, a man who really stands by his word and deed, without letting himself be led by αἰδώς, shame before his own people, and earthly reputation. It is true we must take care not to bring the conflict of principles into the Attic tragedy, and what Karl Reinhardt has advanced against the Hegelian interpretation of *Antigone*[35] is just as valid for the older tragedy.

The figures are richer, more vigorous, their actions and their fates are determined by more colorful motives than can be reduced to abstract concepts. But this much we can set down: the actions of the figures in the tragedies are personal actions, "actions" in the exact sense of the word, genuine decisions. And they are made so by the fact that men are faced with divergent claims each bearing within it the seed both of *hubris* and of genuine right and that the man *can* only choose one alternative, but choose one he must.

This is made especially clear in Aeschylus' dramas where a man stands face to face with two contradicting sacred directives—a situation not found in Homer—such as Orestes whom Apollo commands to kill his mother and thereby violate a sanctified right or Pelasgos whose religious duty it is to give refuge to those beseeching him for protection at the altar while at the same time he runs the risk of violating his kingly duty to care for the well-being and peace of his city.

In this sense an Achilles who decides for himself cannot win our sympathy within the moral framework we find in Homer. We sympathize with the Achilles of Aeschylus only because we are convinced that he by his deeds wants not only to reëstablish his reputation and honor, but to restore a higher order for which he feels himself responsible. His tragedy is that by defending *dike* he violates just this *dike* and so draws all the

---

[35] *Sophokles*, pp. 73 ff. See also E. R. Schwinge, *Hypomnemata*, I, 76 f.

more disaster upon himself and upon those who are dear to him.

This is the new awareness which man has gained of himself and that we have been able to recognize by comparing Aeschylus and Homer.

II

Passion and Reason:
Phaedra in *Hippolytos* I

In *Hippolytos* of Euripides (375 ff.), Phaedra, the wife of Theseus, says in recounting her unhappy love for her own stepson, "In many a long night hour I have meditated on what it is that ruins the life of men, what wrecks it" (ὡς διέφθαρται).

Euripides himself, no doubt, also spent many a night wondering why human beings cannot manage their own lives. In the oldest surviving Euripides tragedies, the life that is "out of joint," the life in which men are destroyed, is the life within the narrow confines of the family circle. In *Alcestis*, of 438 B.C., he asks how the members of a family should behave if they really belong together—and what they actually do when they are put to the test. Alcestis alone passes this test as she is prepared to go to her death for the sake of her husband and brings everything once again to a happy conclusion.

The next play by Euripides that has been preserved also portrays the disintegration of the family. The plot, however, is not taken from a sentimental legend but from a situation in an heroic saga which Euripides develops to its most blatant form: in Medea (431 B.C.), Jason fulfils his duties as husband and father to a lesser degree even than Admetus, the husband of Alcestis. Medea reacts with terrifying passion and murders her children. In a monologue (1077 ff.), she realizes that her passion is stronger than her reason.

Three years later, Phaedra in *Hippolytos* resumes this monologue with the lines quoted at the beginning, and if, as she says,
she has meditated for nights on why the *bios* of men is "out of
joint," we are not surprised when she develops her thoughts
further and gives them universal significance.

It is, however, not only Medea's reflection that Phaedra
continues here. The *Hippolytos* in which this monologue occurs
is a revised version. Euripides had already dealt with Phaedra's
love for her stepson Hippolytos in an earlier drama, likewise
called *Hippolytos*. This drama, *Hippolytos Kalyptomenos*,
"Hippolytos who veils his head" as the play has been called to
distinguish it from *Hippolytos Stephanophoros*, the "wreath
bearer," which has been preserved, has not been handed down
to us, but it is possible to reconstruct large parts of it from
fragments and echoes in other works.

When Phaedra, in the monologue from the extant *Hippolytos*,
states so explicitly what she has discovered in her nocturnal
meditations on the causes of human suffering, it is probably
worthwhile asking what new elements are to be found in this
second Phaedra's reflections. Between the two *Hippolytos* plays
Euripides wrote his *Medea*. Let us compare the second Phaedra
on the one hand with Medea, whose monologue she continues,
and on the other hand with the first Phaedra some of whose
characteristics she preserves, but to some of which she gives
a new significance. It may be that a comparison with *Alcestis*
which seems to be earlier than the first *Hippolytos* will show
that the first Phaedra too had something new to say, and that
later Euripides was engaged in discussions which made his
interpretation of man important for the tenets of Attic philosophy, which was beginning to take shape at the time.

Therefore, in order to understand the second Phaedra better,
we must first establish whether we can discover enough about
the first to make the comparison worthwhile.

Our most important aid in any reconstruction of the first
Hippolytos is Seneca's *Phaedra* which I and many others believe
is based to a large extent on this lost drama of Euripides. But

as this has been doubted recently by eminent scholars it must be reëxamined.

The material that is relevant—and some that is not—has been compiled clearly and reliably in a dissertation by C. Zintzen: *Analytisches Hypomnema zu Senecas "Phaedra."*[1] In a review of this book, Pierre Grimal expresses serious doubts that all parallels which Zintzen draws between Seneca's tragedy and later writers prove that these passages go back to the first *Hippolytos*.[2] In many cases he is no doubt right.[3] A more detailed criticism of the prevalent optimistic assumption that one can learn much about the lost *Hippolytos* from Seneca's drama is given by W. S. Barrett in his commentary on Euripides' *Hippolytos*. Unfortunately this important work has not yet been published, but the author has kindly made available to me the proof sheets and allowed me to use them.

Mr. Barrett is inclined to assume that Sophocles' *Phaedra* influenced Seneca, and he may well be right. But on the other hand I believe we may be sure that the structure of Seneca's play follows the basic structure of Euripides' lost *Hippolytos*. I think that in the questions I am concerned with here, we shall find valuable help from Seneca, although he does not take over the wording of Euripides, but changes, adds, or omits a good deal.

There are several reasons why I confidently rely upon some passages of Seneca.

Seneca has taken one scene (396 ff.) from the second *Hippolytos* (where Phaedra imagines herself hunting together with Hippolytos: 215–222) as has been observed long ago. Barrett

---

[1] *Beiträge zur klassischen Philologie*, ed. by R. Merkelbach, Vol. I, 1960.

[2] *Rev. ét. anc.*, 65, 1963, 210 ff.

[3] But if he says (p. 211): "M. Zintzen et ses devanciers nous assurent que les récits romanesques dans lesquels se trouvent des amours d'une femme impudique . . . se conforment tous au schéma donné une fois pour toutes par Euripide" and if he himself doubts that any certainty is possible in these questions, he undoubtedly goes too far. It is not a matter only "des amours d'une femme impudique," but, as I hope to show, a much more specialized situation that has been brought forward for the first time by Euripides.

rightly says that this scene comes into the play "most ineptly":
"There can be no doubt whence the scene is derived; there can
equally be no doubt, when it has been thus rehashed and thus
misused, that it would be perilous in the rest of the play to use
Seneca as evidence for the detail of a hypothetical model that
is no longer preserved" (p. 36, n. 3).

I should rather draw a different conclusion from the facts.
If a scene taken from a context known to us fits so badly into
Seneca's play, we may assume that the main structure of those
parts that are coherent has been taken over from one single
Attic tragedy. As we know from other dramas of Seneca, he
does not aim at a consequent and logical action or at a coherent
psychology in his characters. So if we can trace back vital
scenes to the first *Hippolytos* it seems probable that other
scenes that fit into the same texture go back to the same
tragedy.

The most important evidence for the Euripidean origin of
the plan of Seneca's *Phaedra* seems to be fr. 430 N.[2] (fr.
C. Barrett) which, so far as I know, has not yet been used in
this context, although I do not claim to know all the literature
on these topics. This fragment runs:

> ἔχω δὲ τόλμης καὶ θράσους διδάσκαλον
> ἐν τοῖς ἀμηχάνοισιν εὐπορώτατον,
> Ἔρωτα, πάντων δυσμαχώτατον θεόν.

"I have a teacher in courage and boldness Eros, him who is the
best help in helplessness, amongst all gods that one it is most
difficult to fight against."

Here Phaedra makes clear that her way leads her from
ἀμηχανία (helplessness) to τόλμη and θράσος (courage and
boldness), and that is exactly what we find in Seneca. At first
she is helpless in her unhappy love but then daringly approaches
Hippolytos to win his love. It is superfluous to say that this
cannot be Sophocles.[4] As I shall show later the special sort of
ἀμηχανία found in Seneca's *Phaedra* has been depicted by

---

[4] Cf. Barrett, p. 12.

Euripides for the first time; this is by no means a conventional
feature of Phaedra that had to turn up with any Phaedra in
poetry.

I agree with Barrett, that fr. 443 N.² (his fr. A) must belong
to the prologue spoken by Phaedra:

> ὦ λαμπρὸς αἰθὴρ ἡμέρας θ' ἁγνὸν φάος,
> ὡς ἡδὺ λεύσσειν τοῖς τε πράσσουσιν καλῶς
> καὶ τοῖσι δυστυχοῦσιν, ὧν πέφυκ' ἐγώ.

"O shining aither and holy light of the day, how sweet to behold
for those that are happy and for those that are unhappy to
whom I belong."

We find nothing corresponding to this in the beginning of
Seneca's play because Seneca likes to surround his characters
when they enter the stage with what one could call a cloud of
their milieu. Thus Hippolytos in the prologue (1–84) evokes
the landscape of Attica, the different kinds of dogs and hunting
tools, the wide realm of Diana—none of this is Euripides.
Similarly, Theseus later enters (835–849) haunted by the terrors
of Hades he has just left, and so Phaedra (85 ff.) has first to
conjure up the atmosphere of her homeland Crete. But then
she says of herself and her unhappiness: *degere aetatem in malis
lacrimisque* and continues (90): *sed maior alius incubat maestae
dolor.* That Seneca dropped the invocation of Aether and Daylight need not worry us either—this is an Athenian stage
convention he neglects.[5]

Barrett takes as the likeliest assumption that Seneca adopted
some motifs from the first *Hippolytos.* For example, Barrett
says (p. 37) about Phaedra's approach to Hippolytos: "the
scene may well be based on the first *Hippolytos,* but how closely
we cannot say." This is the scene which gave to the drama the
name *Hippolytos Kalyptomenos,* because Hippolytos veiled
himself when Phaedra made him her shameless offer. To be
sure, Seneca does not mention the veiling, and he has padded

---

[5] Invocation of the sun or the daylight seems originally to be justified in the first
piece of a tetralogy which in fact was produced on the stage in the early morning.

the scene with much bombastic rhetoric, but there can be no serious doubt that the structure of the scene and the character of Phaedra are taken over from the first *Hippolytos*, because it is precisely this scene that gives rise to the indignation about Phaedra's shamelessness (and a shameless Phaedra is certainly not Sophoclean). Moreover, another trait I shall consider later (p. 34 ff.) confirms this, if confirmation is needed.

Barrett furthermore (p. 36) concedes that the "dialogue (129–273), with Phaedra bent on her love and the Nurse trying vainly to dissuade her . . . may well have been suggested by a Greek model, and the first *Hippolytos* seems the more likely source." Of this we may be sure, although with Barrett we must concede that the alleged verbal resemblances with fragments of the Euripidean play do not prove anything.[6] To this scene, too, I shall return later (p. 38 ff.).

All these examples are relevant episodes in the drama; each is a decisive scene. Hence, I think we may be confident in finding essential elements of the first *Hippolytos* in Seneca's *Phaedra*. This will become even more apparent, if we should find that these motifs were by no means as trivial and conventional for Euripides as they seem to us, who are aware that they have been taken over from Euripides many hundreds of times.

But even if Barrett were right in claiming that the influence of Sophocles' *Phaedra* was greater than I think it was, the considerations I should like to bring forward would not be seriously invalidated, since my main point is to show what is new in *Medea* and in the Phaedra of the second *Hippolytos*. Since Barrett (pp. 29 ff.) is inclined to put Sophocles' *Phaedra* before the second *Hippolytos* of Euripides, passages in Seneca taken from Sophocles would in any case be older than the second *Hippolytos* and probably older than *Medea* too, which

---

[6] A minor point is that the prayer of the nurse to the moon (Sen. 406–423) was "presumably suggested by ['I say: suggested by, not: adapted from,' Barrett says on p. 36, n. 4] Phaedra's prayer to the moon in the first Hippolytos" (fr. E Barr., p. 491 N.²). Other instances will be mentioned below.

was performed only three years before the second *Hippolytos*. So, even if it is difficult indeed to come to a definite judgment about the details, I hope to be on sufficiently firm ground for the present investigation.

In the hypothesis to the extant *Hippolytos* we read, "This is the second *Hippolytos* . . . it is clear that it was written later because the indecent and blameworthy elements [τὸ ἀπρεπὲς καὶ κακηγορίας ἄξιον] have been corrected in this drama." Aristophanes (*Frogs* 1044 Φαίδρας . . . πόρνας etc.[7]) had already reproached Euripides for putting a dissolute female (Phaedra) on the stage, and Euripides is evidently taking this into consideration when he makes the goddess Aphrodite narrate the contents of the new play at the beginning of the second *Hippolytos*. She says of Phaedra (47): "her reputation is irreproachable, but she perishes nevertheless," ἥδ' εὐκλεὴς μέν, ἀλλ' ὅμως ἀπόλλυται. Whether it is his intention here to inform his audience that this time they were to see a more noble Phaedra, or whether he is protesting against a false interpretation of his earlier Phaedra, we shall investigate later.

Seneca gives Phaedra's love for her stepson Hippolytos different motivations, and these were probably to be found in the first version of Euripides' *Hippolytos*. On the one hand, Phaedra attributes her passion to the fact that she is a descendant of Helios (124 ff.): Aphrodite hates and persecutes all descendants of the sun god because he had once published abroad her adultery with Ares. As a result, her mother Pasiphae started an unnatural love affair with the Minotaur, and Phaedra's sister Ariadne fell in love with the national enemy Theseus.

Seneca's Phaedra alludes to this (112) with the words: *fatale miserae matris . . . malum*, her own passion and sickness are inherited from her mother and ordained by the gods;[8] and in a fragment (fr. 444) of Euripides' play, somebody says (probably Phaedra): "O daemon, that for us human creatures

[7] Barrett, Appendix d(a) collects the similar testimonia.
[8] Zintzen p. 18.

there is no defence against the evil born within us and sent by the gods."[9]

This mythical-genealogical motivation can well conform to traditional notions, but Seneca has abridged too much for us to be able to estimate the full effect of the motive in Euripides' first *Hippolytos*. In the second *Hippolytos*, Euripides, as we shall see, gave greater emphasis to the mythical motivation though he altered it radically.

Phaedra mentions, in addition, something different as a motive for her love for Hippolytos—something human, something psychological (92): Theseus has left her, *praestatque nuptae quam solet Theseus fidem*, "Theseus keeps his fidelity as he uses to do." If we read this verse, we expect that Phaedra mentions that Theseus had earlier left her sister Ariadne and that he had other relations with other women. She tries to exculpate herself by contending that Theseus, too, had committed adultery. But surprisingly Phaedra continues (97 f.): *stupra et illicitos toros Acheronte in imo quaerit Hippolyti pater*, "he seeks adultery and forbidden beds in Hades, the father of Hippolytos." But this aims at something different: Theseus helps Peirothoös ravish Persephone, and it is not he who is bent on adultery, but his friend.

Now Plutarch (*Mor.* 27f–28a) says: (Εὐριπίδης) τὴν . . . Φαίδραν καὶ προσεγκαλοῦσαν τῷ Θησεῖ πεποίηκεν ὡς διὰ τὰς ἐκείνου παρανομίας ἐρασθεῖσαν τοῦ Ἱππολύτου, "Euripides made Phaedra make reproaches to Theseus, that she fell in love with Hippolytos on account of his παρανομίαι [his trespassings]" (fr. B Barr., p. 491 N.²) and that would correspond well to 92 in Seneca: "he keeps his fidelity as he uses to do." But in mentioning the adultery of Peirithoös, Seneca apparently gets into a muddle, and this may mean that he wished to let us know

---

[9] Fr. 444 N.² = fr. S Barr.:

ὦ δαῖμον, ὡς οὐκ ἔστ' ἀποστροφὴ βροτοῖς
τῶν ἐμφύτων τε καὶ θεηλάτων κακῶν,

i.e., φύσις and god cause the evil—that this for Euripides is almost one and the same will be evident later.

in time that he makes Theseus absent in Hades and that he did not take this from Euripides.[10] But this much is certain: Euripides in the first *Hippolytos* made Phaedra's love for Hippolytos a kind of revenge against Theseus—though unfortunately we cannot determine the details.

Here thoughts crop up which Aeschylus' Clytemnestra had already expressed. We remember how Clytemnestra in *Agamemnon* told the Chorus that she felt no shame at what she had done or said. Just as Phaedra makes use of Theseus' infidelity to her to excuse her love for Hippolytos, Clytemnestra (1440) accuses Agamemnon of infidelity with Cassandra. This of course implies that she feels justified in indulging in the same kind of thing with Aegisthus. Both, therefore, make use of the age-old right: tit for tat, an eye for an eye. Clytemnestra can go even further than Phaedra in this respect. Agamemnon has sacrificed her daughter Iphigenia; therefore, it is her right to slaughter him (1417, 1432). As I tried to show earlier, man's actions and his awareness of what is right had by this time become problematical. Thus, this ancient, so to speak "quantitative compensation" could no longer be the last word in justice. But though Aeschylus no longer accepts the validity of reprisal, it is still for him an active force in man. The individual's claim to avenge an injustice may be doubtful, but vengeance for vengeance occurs time and time again.

One action may well call forth an even greater counteraction, and this counteraction a still greater, even worse one. This is how Homer in the Iliad explains the causality of events. Agamemnon seizes Chryseis, whereupon her father Chryses beseeches Apollo to send the plague; Agamemnon gives Chryseis back, but takes Briseis; and Achilles sulks in his tent as a result. This kind of thing recurs in many ancient myths, and even Herodotus explains the Grecian wars with the Orient as

---

[10] In fact two fragments show that Sophocles in his *Phaedra* made Theseus absent in Hades (624 f. N., 686 f. P., A and H Barr.); cf. Barrett App., pp. 31 f. Seneca may well have taken over this motif because it gave him the opportunity for Theseus' speech, 835–849.

a slow progression of reprisals executed for one injustice after another.

I do not wish to pursue here how this inevitability of blow and counterblow is connected in Aeschylus' work (and before him) with the belief in a family curse, nor how the succession of such happenings acquires in this way all the more inviolable necessity. Not only Clytemnestra but Achilles as well showed how such necessity becomes problematical since Aeschylus measures actions by an absolute right. In Sophocles it is precisely great men who rebel against the fact that the world, ruled as it is by the law of action and counteraction, is "out of joint." They try to "set it right" again and thereby come to a disastrous end. But this is well known.

Such concepts of an objective settlement both as a genuine and as a purported motive for action, as well as a concatenation in the destiny of a house or family, play a much less important role in Euripides' work than in Aeschylus' or Sophocles'. True, Aphrodite in Seneca's *Phaedra* hates the granddaughter of Helios because he had once disclosed her love for Ares. At least Phaedra says this is so (124–155), but it is scarcely an important factor in the play as a whole. On the earthly plane, certainly, Phaedra's sinful love is motivated as a "counteraction" to her husband's "action," but this motive has much less weight than in the case of Aeschylus' Clytemnestra; Phaedra is much more driven by other motives. With her it is rather a matter of mental "disposition," of "psychology," than an effort to take revenge against Theseus.

As a result, there is a considerable shift both in the "mythical" as well as in the "human" motivation of the action—and this is something basically new. Ever since scholars have started comparing Euripides' women with Ibsen's Hedda Gabler or Nora,[11] it has become a platitude to say that he discovered the female psyche. This is like saying that the female "psyche" is as clearly discernible as, say, the Island of Tahiti, which was suddenly discovered one day. It seems to me we ought to

---

[11] Cf. for example, K. Reinhardt, *Tradition und Geist*, pp. 236 ff.

define more exactly what such a discovery means; then we shall see that the discovery is more exciting and closer to ancient ideas. It is possible to diagnose soberly and exactly which specific emotions Euripides is considering and which conventional motives help him to portray and interpret these emotions.

For this purpose let us now investigate in detail, how those psychological motives which Seneca's Phaedra has, return at decisive moments either identically or at least similarly in the fragments of the lost first *Hippolytos*. In her first speech (85 ff.), Phaedra mentions that the faithless Theseus has left her (91–98). She herself as a granddaughter of the Sun God has to endure the vengeance of Aphrodite who has plunged her, like her mother Pasiphae before her, into an unhappy love affair. Unlike Aeschylus' Clytemnestra, however, she does not directly plan to avenge herself by forcing her stepson Hippolytos to return her love. She is only aware of her misfortune and passes her life in tears (90). Her passion robs her of her sleep and rest (100) and an inner fire consumes her. She can no longer weave, no longer take part in the religious ceremonies (105). These are symptoms of helplessness, similar to those described by Archilochos and Sappho when unhappily in love,[12] symptoms which as far as we know occur here for the first time in tragedy and are here for the first time applied to moral phenomena. We have seen already, that Phaedra in a fragment of the first *Hippolytos* describes her state of mind with the word τὰ ἀμήχανα, a word typical of the early lyrical poets.

Homer interprets questions of right and morals as if they were material possessions. Right (δίκη) and honor (τιμή), which are cardinal in Homer's social order, have to be distributed in appropriate "portions." Everybody must preserve or attain the portion of honor and right which falls to his share, but, on the other hand, he must take care that he does not infringe upon

---

[12] *Entdeck.*[3], pp. 93 ff. For the idle loom see Sappho fr. 102 L.-P. Zintzen quotes each time a large number of parallels to Seneca's verses, especially those that in his opinion suggest Euripides as an origin for the motifs. In general, I am not repeating them, but merely appending those relevant to my context, especially those which concern the first appearances of the motifs.

the due portions of others. Crime, hubris, and insult are en-
croachments on the property of others. Any settlement,
compensation, or indemnification must give back to the injured
party his quantity of right and reputation.

Archilochos and Sappho, on the other hand, are not primarily
concerned with problems of right or morals—or at least not as
they concern their own actions—when they speak of their
ἀμηχανία. For them the tension of their lives, the conflict
between life and death, love and suffering, joy and sorrow is
the primeval phenomenon according to which they interpret
both themselves and others. Helplessness, ἀμηχανία, begins
when in the vicissitudes of the emotions one loses contact with
other men and stands alone. For them it is important to be
united with others in sentiments, disposition, and convictions.[13]
Euripides takes up these motives and extends them.

Before I further develop the most important point, namely,
that for Phaedra this ἀμηχανία is a state of *moral* helplessness,
I should like to show that Phaedra's wish to be together with
Hippolytos has new traits also.

Phaedra says in Seneca's play (110): "My desire is to pursue
the startled game on the run and to hurl hunting spears," and
later (235) she wishes to follow Hippolytos into the snow-
capped mountains. A similar theme recurs (396), but this time
it is certainly taken, as I have pointed out before (p. 26), from
the second *Hippolytos* (215 ff.), where Phaedra in her delirium
dreams up the hunt with Hippolytos. Seneca could, therefore,
have formed the first two passages under the influence of the
third one. But it seems more probable that Euripides in the
second *Hippolytos* developed a motif of the first *Hippolytos* into
a grand vision than that Seneca should have spoiled the surprising effect of these hallucinations by hinting at them beforehand in two remarks of his own invention. Rather he left there
two passages where he found them in the first *Hippolytos*
without being aware that he would introduce this motif later
on in a more impressive form from the second *Hippolytos*.

---

[13] Cf. *Poetry and Society*, pp. 28 ff.

As far as we know, Aeschylus was the first to portray someone making demands over and beyond his form of life, and beginning a new *bios:* the satyrs of his *Isthmiastai* have become sick of their paltry life and want to play at young sportsmen. But this simply means that they want to be better off. Phaedra expresses the desire to share in the life of the one she loves, and she seeks an inner union with the person she loves; this is a motif of archaic lyrics.[14] But she evinces a third motif—something we meet for the first time in Euripides' *Alcestis:*[15] Here Admetus has no "genuine" love of Alcestis; he is helpless in a situation where he ought not to think only of his own life. So the question of genuine companionship acquires a new moral importance: the problem of moral insufficiency arises. Admetos, of course, is far from being unfaithful, but in a definite, sanctioned walk of life he is not fulfilling inwardly what is expected of him. Phaedra tries to overcome this weakness by changing her life, but that remains wishful thinking, an unrealistic fancy.

Certainly, Clytemnestra does not accomplish what one would expect from a good housewife—she even transgresses the holy laws of marriage—but for her, adultery is an act of revenge, not a desire to change her life and to share in the ways of her lover. But the most important difference between Clytemnestra and Phaedra is that Clytemnestra takes the act of reprisal upon herself in the full consciousness of her strength (though this pride ultimately breaks down), whereas Phaedra is at the mercy of her weakness. This is the new "psychological" portrait Euripides draws. In order to achieve this Euripides not only combines different patterns of early Greek thinking, but combines in Phaedra two different figures of older tales. We shall see later that the fable of Phaedra has grown out of a story like that of Bellerophon or of Potiphar's wife, where a woman tries to seduce a chaste young man and after having failed tries to destroy him by calumny.

If the Euripidean Phaedra wishes to be a huntress, she takes

---

[14] See above, p. 34.
[15] *Poetry and Society*, pp. 83 ff.

up motifs from Atalante who is hunting "on the summits of high mountains" (Theognis 1292). But Phaedra is an Atalante in reverse: Atalante by hunting "flees lovely marriage and the gifts of Aphrodite" (Theognis 1293 f.) and lives in the company of Artemis (Eur., *Phoen.* 151). But Phaedra by hunting hopes to win the love of Hippolytos who on his part, like Atalante, is "always," as Aphrodite says in the prologue of Euripides' drama, "living together with the virgin goddess in the green forests."[16]

So, Phaedra is striving for a radical change of her life. We do not know who has first combined Phaedra's illicit love with her wish to hunt like Atalante. Whoever did it had to change the chaste juvenile of the old tale, who was persecuted by a loving woman, to a hunter and so had to assimilate him to Atalante. At any rate, Euripides by combining these two different forms of life in his Phaedra gave her a peculiar inner tension: helpless as she is, in her fever, in her dreams, in her fancies she flees into another existence, and in an eccentric and unrealistic enthusiasm she tries to overcome her moral embarrassment. That is something we can observe in other Euripidean dramas too.

Of course, ever since man has felt the imperfection of this world, he has dreamed of a paradise or of a golden age, and his wish to return there was often combined with an unrealistic enthusiasm. Such fantastic longings to get rid of one's own distress and helplessness and to find a different life occur in various forms in early Greek poetry too. Alcman, for instance, is longing to shake off the burden of old age and wants to become a seabird who is easily carried over the waves (fr. 26 Page).

But the exaltation of Phaedra and of cognate characters in Euripides differs from those older examples: it is much more connected with personal action, be it to the good or to the bad.

---

[16] One might suppose that this combination of hunting and loving had something to do with the notion that Eros wears bow and arrows, but this does not occur before the fourth century B.C.

Fantastic though their imaginations may be, these do not merely pass before the inner eye as nonobliging phantasmagoriae but have an immediate impact upon what the person is going to do.

We shall better leave aside the question of whether Euripides herewith discovers something characteristic of the human or especially of the female soul. Certainly female characters as Alcestis, the two Phaedras, Medea (and later Makaria in the *Herakleidai*) are important for the development of such ideas, but male figures too in his dramas like Menoikeus show similar traits.

May I mention by way of digression that this Phaedra who wants to go hunting has had a curious "after-life." It has become an established literary "topos," that a person, and especially a woman, in unhappy love wants to go hunting.

In Vergil (*Ecl.* 10, 56), Gallus in his unhappy love wants to hunt boars (this special feature comes from Atalante), Sulpicia (Tibullus 3, 9, 11) wishes to hunt in order to be together with Cerinthus, in Ovid's *Metamorphoses* (10, 535 ff.) even Venus wants to be a huntress and to join Adonis, and in his *Heroides* (4, 38 ff.) Phaedra writes to Hippolytos what she had said on her fever bed in Euripides' drama (215 ff.). That Seneca in his *Phaedra*, following Euripides, took up this motif not less than three times (110, 235, 396) I have said before (and in line 233 he combines it with Verg., *Ecl.* 10, 47).

When in modern literature life without love is a huntress' life, it is usually the situation of Atalanta and not that of Phaedra that is depicted. But if the girl who wants to remain chaste speaks herself, in her own words, of her wish to hunt, at least this goes back to Euripides' *Phaedra*. So Chaucer (*Cant. Tales* 2307 f.) makes Emilia say: *I am, thou woost, yet of thy compaignye,/ A mayde, and love huntynge and venerye.* And Tasso's Silvia, before falling in love with Aminta, assures:

> me questa vita giova, e 'l mio trastullo
> è la cura de l'arco e de gli strali;
> seguir le fere fugaci, e le forti

atterrar combattendo; e se non mancano
saette a la faretra, o fere al bosco,
non tem' io che a me manchino diporti.

Whether Seneca took the idea that Phaedra wanted to join
Hippolytos on the hunt from the first or the second *Hippolytos*
may not be clear, but at least the pathological state which
makes the Phaedra of the second version say such a thing is
equally characteristic of the Phaedra of the first play. Seneca's
Phaedra is also perfectly aware of the fact that her life, to use
the words of the second Phaedra, is destroyed (διέφθαρται),
that she is entangled in an unfortunate love-affair, even though
she may not diagnose her sickness herself—*not yet* diagnose it
herself as we can say in view of the second Phaedra as we shall
see later. But in Seneca, and accordingly in the first *Hippolytos*
of Euripides, she rather realizes her condition from the remon-
strances of her nurse (177): "I know that what you say is true.
But passion forces me to follow the bad one . . . "; (184):
"What is the good of reflection? Passion is victorious and rules
the day; the god (Amor) reigns supreme in my whole heart."
    Zintzen (pp. 25 and 27) compares these words to fragments
433 (P Barr.) and 431 (Soph., *Phaedra*, fr. B Barr.) of the first
Hippolytos, but neither is any help to us. Fragment 433 reads:
"I maintain one should never respect a law more than is
necessary when one is in misfortune." If, as Zintzen and others
suppose, these words are spoken by Phaedra, it would, at the
very least, mean that she knows herself to be in a predicament
(ἐν τοῖσι δεινοῖς). But it is also possible that they are spoken by
the nurse in an attempt to encourage her mistress to dare the
utmost (*dicit qui scelus suadet*, Wilamowitz wrote in his working
copy) or, as Barrett suggests, by Hippolytos or Theseus. Fragment 431 says: "Eros attacks not only men and women, but
confuses[17] also the souls of the gods and reaches across the
seas. Even the almighty Zeus cannot repulse him with his
power, but yields and submits willingly." It is improbable that

---

[17] ταράσσει Clemens, χαράσσει Stob.

these lines were even written by Euripides; Clemens, it is true, ascribes them to him, but Stobaios names Sophocles as the author (fr. 684 Pearson = fr. B Barr.). Indeed, they contain nothing characteristic either of Euripides or of the particular position in which Phaedra finds herself; they merely say that Eros has power also over the gods, a fact of which both Sophocles and Euripides were perfectly aware.[18] Nothing forces us to assume that Phaedra speaks these words, nor even that she speaks them in a state of helpless desperation, as Seneca's Phaedra confesses (184): "I am governed by my passion, and the mighty god holds sway over my whole heart."

However, fragment 430 (C Barr.) takes us further: "As tutor in courage and boldness [indeed, insolence: τόλμης καὶ θράσους], as the one who knows the best way out of helplessness [ἐν τοῖς ἀμηχάνοισιν] I have Eros, the god who is the most difficult to combat of all." These words are beyond doubt spoken by Phaedra, namely after she has decided to confess her passion to Hippolytos and win his love in return. To be sure, these words have no exact parallel in Seneca's play,[19] but they fit precisely into the plot of his drama. Phaedra speaks of her helplessness. The word ἀμήχανος in ancient poetry designates precisely that condition, the portrayal of which links Euripides with the archaic poets; in this condition we find Phaedra at the beginning of Seneca's play; this condition as a psychological point of departure (as will be confirmed later) is new and typical in Euripides' early tragedies. That is why I consider it so improbable that Seneca should not have followed Euripides when he wrote his play. The subsequent action of Seneca's tragedy also fits in well with these words from Euripides' first *Hippolytos*. Phaedra wants Eros as her tutor in courage and boldness; she calls him Eros εὔπορος, "the one who finds ways out" from helplessness (Plato takes this thought

[18] Further passages quoted by Pearson in his notes to Soph. fr. 941, 13.
[19] Zintzen, p. 30, links the words up with Sen. *Phaedra* 218: *amoris in me maximum regnum fero, reditusque nullos metuo*, but here neither the resoluteness nor the helplessness is so clearly expressed, and, so far, Barrett (p. 36) is perfectly right.

up in the Diotima speech of the *Symposium*). Indeed, she does not lack courage to do what she has to do. Seneca treats the transition from helplessness to boldness thus: After Phaedra in her first speech (85–127) portrays herself as one overcome by passion, the nurse admonishes her (128–177) to suppress her impious lust. She cannot rely on Theseus not returning and her love remaining a secret; at least she would suffer under the consciousness of her guilt. The nurse is the first *confidante* on the European stage, the ancestor of many characters especially of French drama. In Seneca she plays the warner who, for instance in Herodotus, is a standing figure who maintains sound judgment before the ambitious aspirations of a ruler. Phaedra answers (177–194) that she is incapable of resisting Amor. The nurse retorts (195–217) that it is an affront to declare passion to be a god and to excuse oneself thereby; people who are prosperous are all too prone to direct their wishes to the unusual, the exorbitant. Phaedra replies (218–222): "It is true that I am governed completely by Amor; Theseus' return I do not fear." In the dialogue that follows she at first insists, despite all objections put forward by the nurse, on winning Hippolytos' love,[20] only suddenly to declare that if she wanted to preserve her reputation, all she could do would be to take her own life. This wins the nurse to her side, and she then undertakes to win Hippolytos over for her mistress (271 ff.).

Seneca has altered, abridged, emphasized, and given a Stoical-philosophical twist to many details, but the whole scene is in itself coherent, and at least one important idea can probably be traced back to the first *Hippolytos* of Euripides. So it becomes even more evident that Euripides—even in the first version—had motivated Phaedra's actions not solely as a reaction to an action which befalls her but deduced it from her psychological state of mind.

According to the nurse, it is *luxuria* that makes Phaedra crave for exorbitance (204 f.). Two sentences from the first

---

[20] On the text of 239 f., cf. H. Fuchs, *Hermes*, 70, 1935, 247.

Hippolytos, presumably[21] spoken by the nurse read: "I see that in general previous prosperity begets *hubris* in mankind." (fr. 437 = L Barr.) and (fr. 438 = M Barr.), "Wealth ⟨is more likely⟩ to beget ⟨passion⟩ and *hubris* than a meager way of life."[22] True, there is nothing new about the idea of a man who is too well off lapsing into *hubris*. Tantalus is a good example. Solon also demonstrates in the old story to Croesus that the simple life can bring a more secure form of happiness than power, reputation, and wealth. As a result, the lines we are considering do not sound different from what we hear, for instance, in the poems of Solon. But in these old tales and in the exhortations of the early elegiac poets, *hubris* means the desire for more when one is already prosperous; it incites men to immoderate actions. In the first *Hippolytos*, however, Phaedra's condition was described as exactly the opposite, as ἀμηχανία, as helplessness. Here is a new, a singular situation, the same situation, however, in which we meet Phaedra in Seneca's play. We may therefore assume that Euripides in both fragments connected wealth with *hubris* and developed the two motives in the same way as Seneca was to do later.

But in fact the nurse in Seneca does not so much call *hubris* a consequence of wealth, but rather of *luxuria* (204 f.): "*quisquis secundis rebus exultat nimis/ fluitque luxu, semper insolita appetit.*" This idea too goes back to early elegy: Xenophanes said that wealth had brought the Colophonians to τρυφή, and this seems to be appropriate to the situation of Phaedra. Indeed Barrett has said that, "ὕβρις is a word more suited to Hippolytos' alleged behaviour than to Phaedra's passion"[23]

---

[21] Though Barrett doubts it. But once we admit that Seneca follows the first *Hippolytos*, it is natural to connect fragments of this drama with verses of Seneca's *Phaedra* that are similar to them. Concerning another argument of Barrett's see note 23.

[22] ὕβριν τε τίκτει πλοῦτος ἢ φειδὼ βίου. Evidently something has to be supplied before the extant line such as μᾶλλον πάθη ⟨κόρον⟩ or ἔρωτα μᾶλλον ... Barrett takes up Nauck's οὐ for ἤ. The Syrian translation of Themistios' π. ἀρετῆς quoting this verse (J. Gildemeister and F. Bücheler, *Rh. M.*, 27, 1872, 453) ". . . dass Reichtum Übermut erzeugt und Armut Geld sammelt," is too inaccurate to draw conclusions from it.

[23] App., p. 20, n. 4.

and therefore doubts that the two fragments with τίκτειν ὕβριν were applied to Phaedra, as Leo suggested. But then we get into another difficulty: If the behavior of Hippolytos perhaps might be called *hubris*, it certainly does not stem from his wealth: the chaste hunter leads a primitive life. I propose therefore a different solution: it is only natural that Seneca dwells on the luxury, the τρυφή of the queen, because that is a social problem at his time and a usual topic of his Stoic philosophy. Euripides on the other hand may very well have spoken of τρυφή in verses that have not come down to us, but may have taken up the concept of *hubris* from older stories, where, as in Clytemnestra, illicit love was depicted as *hubris*.[24]

Seneca's nurse, however, not only cautions against the dangers of wealth, as did the old elegiac poets, but goes one step further and praises poverty: the simple nurse extols the simple life almost as a matter of moral principle. This is new for the fifth century, but Euripides develops it in later plays.[25] This moralization of the motives goes even further. We shall come back to it later (p. 87).

When Seneca's Phaedra eventually does confess her love to Hippolytos—I shall not go into details here, for even Barrett concedes that this scene may well be based on the first *Hippolytos*—she advances another reason for this love (646): "I love

[24] Another reason why Barrett doubts that the two fragments could be drawn here is the following: "I do not see how in such a context one could avoid giving both fragments to the nurse, and that the repeated τίκτειν ὕβριν makes this improbable." But that is valid only if we accept the conjecture of Nauck οὐ for ἤ in fr. 438 (M Barrett). The dialogue between the nurse and Phaedra may, for instance, have been:
Nurse (fr. 437): I see that for most people prosperity begets *hubris*.
⟨Phaedra: But Hippolytos in his simple life shows more *hubris*.⟩
Nurse (fr. 438): ⟨Yet⟩ wealth ⟨is more likely⟩ to beget ⟨passion⟩ and hubris than a meagre way of life.
I mention this only to show that it seems not impossible to get over the difficulties mentioned by Barrett.
[25] Examples: Stob. 4, 31, 3 (ψόγος πλούτου) and 4, 32, 1 (ἔπαινος πενίας) but none pre-Euripides. The distichon Theogn. 605 f., which resembles frr. 437 and 438 so closely: πολλῷ τοι πλέονας λιμοῦ κόρος ὤλεσεν ἤδη ἄνδρας, ὅσοι μοίρης πλεῖον ἔχειν ἔθελον, extends the Tantalus experience (cf. also 693 f.). Euripides does not seem to have known the *topos* of the "little hut" which is repeated so often later (Sen. 208 ff. *tecta sani moris aut vilis scyphus, penates . . . tenues, parvis . . . in tectis*).

the countenance of Theseus—the countenance he bore when first he came to Crete." Merkelbach has demonstrated[26] that this is no invention of Seneca's: in Heliodor's novel *Aithiopiaka* (1, 10), Knemon relates that when Demainete saw him for the first time, she ran up to him passionately and embraced him with the words: "My Hippolytos, thou second Theseus".[27]

As Seneca could not possibly have used Heliodor for this passage or for any other of the many corresponding passages, both writers must have had recourse to the same model— namely, as is generally accepted, the first *Hippolytos* of Euripides.[28] This passage assumes therefore particular importance. In it, a woman says she loves a young man because she recognizes in him the father whom she had loved in years gone by. This is, as far as I know, the first example of one person giving a reason for loving another particular individual. Such psychological, personal motivation remained rare in later Greek literature; before Euripides it was unheard of.

On the rare occasions that Homer speaks of the reasons for one human being loving another, it is always the recognized physical characteristics and the conventional virtues that arouse desire and yearning. Whenever, after Homer, someone in archaic times gives reasons for loving a particular person, everything is kept strictly within narrow limits and in the typical formulae of the time. Thus, for example, Sappho emphasizes the simplicity, the unpretentiousness, of the maiden she loves (fr. 16 L.–P.) and Anacreon addresses a girl in the usual animal comparison of the time, as a Thracian foal (fr. 417 Page). This motive, that Phaedra sees in Hippolytos the young Theseus, is particularly apt, of course, for emphasizing the sinfulness of her love for her stepson. This meant a great deal to Euripides, for here he was also intent on doing something new. As such, of course, it is a common enough motif for

[26] *Rh. Mus.*, 100, 1957, 99; cf. Zintzen, pp. 77 f.

[27] ὁ ἐμὸς ‘Ιππόλυτος, ὁ Θησεὺς ὁ νέος (Merkelbach's version of the ms. ‘ὁ νέος ‘Ιππόλυτος, ὁ Θησεὺς ὁ ἐμός).

[28] Theoretically it might go back to Sophocles' *Phaedra*, but such "psychological" motivation is certainly more Euripidean than Sophoclean.

passionate love to run counter to convention. The criminal
love of Stheneboia for Bellerophon, or Clytemnestra's love for
Aegisthus, or even Pasiphae's love for the bull are all examples.
The mythical and literary topos that passionate love is sinful
love, or, seen from the poet's eye, that the passionate element
of love can best be demonstrated in a sinful love affair, runs
through the entire world literature up to *Lady Chatterly* or
Lolita.

The way in which Seneca develops this motive in the rest of
the play—and again manifestly with close reference to the
first *Hippolytos* of Euripides—demonstrates particularly clearly
what Euripides intended.

After Phaedra threatens to commit suicide and the nurse
declares herself prepared to win Hippolytos for her mistress
(271 f.), Seneca admittedly deviates from the first *Hippolytos*
at some length. First, the Chorus indulges in speculations on
the omnipotence of love (274–357); the next scene (358–405) is
based on the second *Hippolytos*. We can ignore that here. With
line 405, Seneca returns to the action of the first *Hippolytos*.

The nurse[29] prays to the goddess of the moon for help. This
certainly corresponds to a scene in the first *Hippolytos* (*Schol.
Theocr.* 2, 10).[30] When Hippolytos enters, she tries to persuade
him to abandon his chaste way of life and follow the natural
dictates of love. Hippolytos, in turn, praises the simple life of
nature. Then Phaedra rushes in and collapses in a faint in his
arms. As soon as she recovers, she sends the Chorus and the
nurse away,[31] and then, in a famous scene, confesses little by
little her love to her stepson.

Hippolytos, horrified, draws his sword, drops it, however,
at once, and runs off (718). The nurse, who must have been
eavesdropping, immediately raises the hue and cry (βοή) pre-

[29] Zintzen, p. 50.

[30] See p. 28, n. 6.

[31] Zintzen, p. 38, lets only the chorus exit, but in line 600 *siquis est abeat comes* must
include the nurse. She cannot possibly be present during the ensuing conversation,
although in line 719 she is admittedly at once on the spot again and knows what has
been happening.

scribed for murder, assault, and rape—first to call for help but
at the same time to proclaim that a deed of violence had been
done. Thereby the nurse initiates the defamation which
Phaedra then endorses before Theseus who returns at that
moment from the Underworld. His sword that he has left
behind offers proof. Theseus immediately curses his son Hippolytos. Poseidon had once promised to grant his son, Theseus,
three wishes. Theseus now makes use of the third and last:
his son shall die (945 ff.). Shortly afterward the messenger
enters and narrates Hippolytos' horrifying end. As he was
riding out of the city in his chariot, a gruesome monster
appeared out of the sea; the horses shied, and Hippolytos was
caught up in the reins as he fell and dragged to his death. In
the last act, Phaedra appears, accusing herself. She alone is to
blame for everything. She falls on the sword. Theseus, in his
despair, arraigns the gods, makes preparations for the burial
of his son, and curses Phaedra.

I shall pass over the details of the action as well as the
question of how far they can be ascribed to the first *Hippolytos*.[32] There may be differences between Seneca and the first
Hippolytos in how the catastrophe came about, but the catastrophe occurred in Euripides too, at least in a similar way. Our
main concern is the character of Phaedra, the way in which
Euripides motivates her actions; and in this respect Seneca
does not deviate from the first *Hippolytos*. Her moral helplessness, her way from helplessness to boldness, then back to
helplessness and suicide in the dramatic scenes of the second
part of the drama and the psychological motivation of her
attitude and actions show that Euripides already in the first
Hippolytes is deeply concerned with the problem of which the
Phaedra of the second *Hippolytos* speaks: she had spent many
a long night in thought on why life, especially life in the family,
is destroyed.

Thus it is no miracle that Euripides even in the first version
of this subject throws the seductress, and not the chaste youth

[32] Cf. Barrett, pp. 38 f., App.

whom she tries to seduce, into much stronger relief than she occupies in those versions of the story which have come down to us from the Orient and which in one way or other are connected with the Phaedra saga. Phaedra's love for Hippolytos and her attempt to avenge herself on him when he spurns her by defaming him before her husband has its closest parallels in the story of Potiphar's wife in Genesis 39. The ancient Egyptian tale "The Two Brothers" also shows a close kinship with Seneca's *Phaedra* and, therefore, with the first *Hippolytos* of Euripides.[33]

But there are remarkable differences. In neither is there anything about mental distress or moral conflict on the part of the seductress. The Bible says that Potiphar's wife "cast her eyes upon Joseph; and she said, lie with me." The Egyptian story reads: "She desired to know him as a woman knows a man, she stood up and put her arms out to him and said, 'Come, let us enjoy an hour and sleep.'" This idea occurs for the first time in Greek literature in the Bellerophontes story in the *Iliad* (6, 160), and it also says only that Anteia in her passion was intent on being united with Bellerophon in secret.

Of the lost *Phaedra* drama of Sophocles we know almost nothing, and so we cannot tell whether his Phaedra resembled Aeschylus' Clytemnestra, who was intent only on avenging an injustice received or whether she already had some of the pathological traits found in Euripides' Phaedra.

Certainly, it is not a very wide area of the female soul Euripides has laid bare for the first time in the lost *Hippolytos*— and one might doubt whether it is characteristic of the female soul alone. The essential point is that he extends the old lyrical ἀμηχανία of passion to moral frailty and that he lets Phaedra become conscious of the consequences of this inner disposition. But that does not mean that he depicts a full female character: Phaedra rather concentrates all her thought on one single concern, namely, to win the love of Hippolytos.

[33] Papyrus Orbiney (Brit. Mus.); G. Lefebvre, *Romans et Contes Égyptiens*, Paris, 1949, 140 ff. It is remarkable that in this story, too, the women threaten to commit suicide. See also Zintzen, pp. 39 ff.

III

Passion and Reason:
Medea and Phaedra in
Hippolytos II

WE HAVE TRIED to establish what we know
about the lost first version of Euripides' *Hippolytos* and concluded that Euripides was the first to paint a psychological
portrait of human moral weakness. His depiction of Phaedra
was significant for the conception of man in later times and has
remained so to the present day.

That man is weak is not a novel discovery. Since Homer's
time, whenever man in general has been the subject of discussion, the qualities that distinguish him from the gods—his
mortality, his frailty, the fact that he passes like the leaves of
the forest (*Il.* 6, 146), that he is the dream of a shadow (Pind.,
P. 8, 95)—have been the predominant thoughts. This feeling
of man's inadequacy increases in late archaic times at the same
rate as man's confidence in his own ability and intellect grows.
This is especially true since Aischylos taught man to be responsible for his own actions; thus on the one hand the pride in his
own achievements increases, but on the other hand, by the
greater burden man now has to bear, his uncertainty and his
anxiety are intensified. Now weakness is interpreted morally—
that is, one can no longer tolerate it as a natural human
deficiency, as an unavoidable fact, but one must overcome it
by one's own moral efforts.[1]

---

[1] *Poetry and Society*, p. 52.

The decisive achievement of Euripides in this respect is that he makes single characters reflect upon their own moral insufficiency. In his oldest preserved tragedy Admetus says, after realizing that Alcestis has sacrificed her life for him (939): ἐγὼ δ' ὃν οὐ χρῆν ζῆν, παρεὶς τὸ μόρσιμον λυπρὸν διάξω βίοτον· ἄρτι μανθάνω. He now realizes that he ought to have taken death upon himself and not having done so, he must lead a dreary life; and he bewails his loneliness, ἐρημία (944) and the loss of his good reputation (959 ff.). Admetus gains this insight into his moral weakness *after* he fails to live up to what one could expect from a true husband. In the first *Hippolytos* Euripides develops this motive further: here Phaedra is conscious of her failure even before she acts. Her "helplessness" is a state of mind that seizes her from the beginning, and she knows beforehand that what she desires is morally dubious.

We shall see that Euripides' Medea is even more aware of her moral ἀμηχανία and more still the second Phaedra. Both, in their monologues, give an exact psychological analysis of their sorrow. In *Orestes* Euripides for the first time names this disposition: conscience, σύνεσις (396: ὅτι σύνοιδα δείν' εἰργασμένος).

It may be noted, incidentally, that Seneca's Phaedra according to this development fits in exactly between the Admetus and the Medea of Euripides, and so it does not seem hazardous to identify her in broad outline with the Phaedra of the first *Hippolytos*, which in all probability was written between the Alcestis and the Medea.

To say that the Greek drama of the fifth century develops further the theme of man's consciousness of his actions, of the motives within his mind in a definite direction, does not, of course, mean that from year to year, from play to play, there are individual tiny advances. The process is much more complicated. It is, however, possible to point to the differences as they occur in plays which stage a similar kind of action and to pursue the stages of the development. Of course, we must always take into consideration unknown plays that have been lost, and the latest stage of the development is not always apparent in a certain tragedy. Of course literary life in ancient Greece was far richer than we imagine; but, for instance, knowing nothing about Euripides' first *Hippolytos* and his *Medea*, one could nevertheless show that in the second *Hippolytos* motifs appear that are not yet found in *Alcestis*, and we could see the development, less perfectly, surely, but not wrongly. But two points ought to be stressed. Firstly, this process is an increase of man's knowledge of man and not merely a change of mood or sentiment. Therefore it makes sense to follow up these new discoveries bit by bit. Secondly it is especially appropriate to suppose that Euripides won his discernment in this field gradually, since he makes his second Phaedra say that only after long nights of thinking did she come to her conclusions. It has often been said that we cannot expect a straightforward one-rail development in Greek tragedy (or in lyric poetry). But the question is not what we can expect but what we actually find—and there, I am afraid, we sometimes really find a steady progress of certain motifs in certain works. I personally confess that I am more happy than unhappy about this, because, in my opinion, this can give us the confidence to understand better the trend of history—and, moreover, to appreciate the importance of poetry as it reveals new aspects of human life.

A closer examination of such achievement reveals as a rule that man reaches new stages of awareness by combining old motifs and that various traditional patterns of thought become interlaced. We have observed, to quote only one example, the process whereby the first Phaedra of Euripides gains consciousness of her situation. She combines the epic concept of right and honor, which deals, as it were, with concrete objects—with the lyrical idea of inner tensions, or the conflict between lively aspiration and helplessness. We have also seen how the dramatic element of self-assertive action and personal responsibility supervenes in order to produce Phaedra's specific intellectual constitution. The psychological interpretation of her actions is decisively new, but this novelty is made possible by the merging and recombining of previously established forms. As a result, man's increasing consciousness reveals a peculiar kind of economy: what is new is not born of nothing, but develops from tradition, from the reinterpretation of old "topoi." This can be traced back to the origin of all reflection, the structure of language. Man can speak only in a language as it is. If he wants to say something new, he has to transform the existing words, metaphors, and sentence structures by changing them according to analogies taken from other forms of speech.[2]

This peculiar trick of the mind of subsisting and renewing itself by saying, so to speak, to the subsistence available: *you* I shall take, but I shall take another in addition, and *you* I prefer to leave to one side—this peculiar trick becomes manifest when men begin to ponder on their own lives, since they consciously reflect on ways to overcome their afflictions and sufferings. Therefore, we can also study this particularly clearly in the way in which Euripides develops his thoughts on the causes of the destruction of human life. In 431 B.C., Euripides' Medea continues the reflection which the Phaedra of the first *Hippolytos* had initiated.[3] In *Medea* as in the two earlier plays by Euripides, *Alcestis* and *Hippolytos I*, life in the family is shattered. Jason has brought back with him to Greece the barbarian woman who had saved his life while helping him to win the Golden Fleece in the far north-east, in Kolchis. He has two children by her. In Corinth, he now wants to marry the daughter of King Creon in order to provide a normal life of security for himself but also for Medea and their children. This, however, hurts Medea to the quick and she takes her revenge by murdering their two children.

Euripides, therefore, takes up the old Clytemnestra motif

---

[2] I have spoken of "Verschränkungen" (interlacings) of grammatical forms in my book *Der Aufbau der Sprache*.

[3] In the following, I do not deal in detail with the plots of *Medea* and *Hippolytos Stephanophoros*. For material relevant to this discussion, see *Entdeckung*[3], 172–178. My chief concern here I have sketched briefly in *Philologus*, 97, 1948, 125–135 which is now superseded by this chapter.

again whereby a woman takes revenge on her husband for an insult—a process in which one deed incites a more drastic counter-deed. But Medea differs from Clytemnestra in that she directs her deed not only against her husband but also against herself. She does not requite like with like, but kills the children which are not only Jason's but also her own. Such self-destruction continues what Aeschylus had been the first to portray in his Achilles and to which Sophocles, shortly after *Medea*, was to give validity for all time in his *Oedipus Rex*. Medea differs, however, both from Aeschylus' Achilles and Sophocles' Oedipus in that she does not act in ignorance of the consequences of her action. She already knows *before* her deed that she will be injuring herself; she knows that she is facing a decision—just as for the first time Aeschylus' Orestes or Pelasgos had to win through to a decision, and this decision is prepared, as in Pelasgos, in a monologue.

Despite the Aeschylean motifs, the significant fact remains that Euripides here develops further the psychological discernment he had arrived at in the first *Hippolytos*. Like Phaedra, Medea is also under the compulsion of a calamitous passion. She, too, is in the clutches of something which she herself cannot acknowledge morally; she, too, is inhibited because she knows that her deed is wicked. By resorting to the Aeschylean elements, Euripides directs the action of his play toward the great monologue in which Medea dissects with trenchant clarity what for Phaedra had evidently been nothing but torture and distress. In the first *Hippolytos*, there was evidently no room for such clear-headed self-analysis.[4] When Phaedra progressed from helplessness (ἀμηχανία) to boldness (τόλμη, θράσος: fr. 430), she was influenced in strong measure by momentary impulses, the behavior of the nurse, and the presence of the young Hippolytos. This now takes a subordinate place: Medea

---

[4] Later (p. 63 f.), we shall meet several other lines of Euripides which contain similar reflections. They were evidently systematically collected by the Stoic Chrysippus and later found their way into various anthologies and treatises. The lines from *Medea* are the earliest among them; this is also proof that Euripides had evidently not had such thoughts before *Medea*.

performs an almost clinical self-diagnosis before she accomplishes her monstrous deed. The immediate reaction gives way to a mediate one.

Her decisive words are:

> νικῶμαι κακοῖς.
> καὶ μανθάνω μέν, οἷα δρᾶν μέλλω κακά,
> θυμὸς δὲ κρείσσων τῶν ἐμῶν βουλευμάτων,
> ὅσπερ μεγίστων αἴτιος κακῶν βροτοῖς.

"I am overcome by evil, and I realize what evil I am about to do, but my θυμός [my agitation, my passion] is stronger than my βουλεύματα [sound considerations] that thymos which is to blame for the greatest evils that men commit." The conflict, therefore, is a battle inside the heart of man. Passion, θυμός,[5] is stronger than the reasonable intentions (βουλεύματα). That is nothing new to us; but here it is making its first appearance. With Aeschylus, in whose works man was first confronted by genuine decisions, it was between valid claims that he had to choose. It was a matter of definite duties which one had to and wanted to take upon oneself: saving the city, granting protection to suppliants, helping other men, avenging one's father, or punishing some other injustice. There, one could talk of a battle so far as various legal maxims or legal concepts were at variance with one another,[6] or, if the situation was interpreted in the traditional mythical way, when there was a dispute between various gods. We shall see that Euripides takes this up again in the second *Hippolytos*, even though he varies it considerably. In the first *Hippolytos*, neither discord among the gods nor inner conflict played a decisive role.

The metaphors of the inner battle occur for the first time in Archilochos (fr. 7 D.) where he says that in the face of suffering there was the stronger, victorious endurance, submission, the κρατερὴ τλημοσύνη (κρατερός has comparative character, κράτος is superior force, victory). It is true that Archilochos at

---

[5] On the meaning of the word in this context, see p. 54 f.
[6] Cf., for example, Aesch., *Eum.* 974 νικᾷ δ᾽ἀγαθῶν ἔρις ἡμετέρα διὰ παντός.

first says (6) that the gods had given mankind such a victorious
firmness in the face of necessity as a remedy, but then he issues
a challenge for this battle with the imperative τλῆτε (10),
"persevere." True, here it is not a moral goal—a struggle, for
instance, between desire and insight—that is under discussion
but the restraint of passionate emotions. There are examples
of this in Homer as well. Homer, however, does not use the
metaphor of the battle but that of the bolting animal that one
restrains. What we understand, since Euripides, as the conflict
between impulse and insight, Homer sees as follows: when the
thymos of man, or his heart, or his urge (μένος) revolts and
threatens to bolt, one can subdue it (δαμνᾶν) or restrain it
(ἐρύκειν) just as one reins in a horse. When Odysseus on the
eve of the slaughter of the suitors hears the suitors laughing
and enjoying themselves with the serving girls, his *thymos* rises
in his breast, as Homer (*Od.* 20, 9) says, and he considers
(πολλὰ δὲ μερμήριζε κατὰ φρένα καὶ κατὰ θυμόν) whether he
should not at once run in among them and kill them. Then his
heart barks within him, but he says, "persevere, heart"
τέτλαθι δή, κραδίη (18)—a phrase which brings us close indeed
to the words of Archilochos although, of course, there is no
mention of the battle metaphor (κρατερή).[7] And so it is that
an emotion, an urge (impulse) of the heart can make itself
independent, so to speak, and, given full rein, plunge man into
disaster. Needless to say, insight is necessary in order to curb
this wild animal, but Homer does not describe any of these
phenomena as a battle between reason and impulse or as an
inner conflict. This image of the subdued animal can comprise
only the irrational, the dangerous, the uncanny elements in
human action, while the element of reason, of planning, appears
only in its negative function as a hindrance and prevention of

---

[7] In the other passages in Homer where the imperative "persevere" occurs (τέτλαθι,
τετλάτω, τλῆτε, (ἐπι) τλήτω) it is directed toward another person. This is even further
from the idea of an inner conflict. When it is addressed toward the heart (κραδίη) of
the other man (*Il.* 19, 220 = 23, 591 τῷ τοι ἐπιτλήτω κραδίη, 16, 275 σὸν δὲ φίλον
κῆρ τετλάτω ἐν στήθεσσιν), it is because this is the organ that helps to stand firm and to
remain calm.

disaster. Homer's concept, in short, comes more or less down to this: whenever one follows his *thymos*, one stumbles blindly into misfortune and can only submissively ascertain that one's ϑυμός was stronger than oneself was—unless, and this is the way in which Homer explains wise actions, a friendly god incites the *thymos* to perform a heroic deed or inspires with clever thoughts.

A genuine activity of the mind, a struggle for a moral decision, can only be properly understood through the image of the inner battle, in which there is victory and defeat. Though Archilochos persists in the Homeric concepts whereby the *thymos* should not be allowed free rein, and although he does not yet interpret the inner conflict in the ethical sense, the battle metaphor, however modest it may be, does provide other possibilities for appealing to the inner activity of man.

Heraclitus, who has many points of contact with Archilochus, uses the metaphor in the same sense: ϑυμῷ μάχεσϑαι χαλεπόν· ὃ γὰρ ἂν ϑέλῃ, ψυχῆς ὠνεῖται "fighting with the *thymos* is difficult because what it would like it buys at the cost of the soul [the life]." Here, not two inner endeavors face each other, but man opposes his *thymos* in much the same way as in Homer— but the call to battle, as in Archilochus, rouses an inner activity.

This image of the inner battle to which Euripides' Medea gives full meaning for the first time by connecting it with a moral conflict (or, in other words: with the aid of this metaphor, she is able to analyze her situation clearly) is subsequently the model by which one orientates oneself when engaged in moral reflection. "Self-command," "victory over self"—these are categories which have been handed down to us, chiefly by way of Socrates and of the Stoa. Medea asks how actions without sense are possible and discovers something that Plato later calls ἐπιϑυμία, "passion."[8] She uses the Homeric word *thymos* that offered itself, naturally enough, in such a context, since the epic described similar scenes with phrases like ϑυμῷ εἴκειν, to give way to one's *thymos*. But this metaphor of the taming

---

[8] This word occurs for the first time in Herodotus in the meaning of "wish."

of an animal is different, as I have said. And *thymos* in Homer is
rather the singular, momentary emotion and not the inner
force of passion that is like a perpetual motor working within
man. This meaning of *thymos* we find for the first time in the
sentence of Heraclitus just quoted, where the *thymos* is the
ever-present adversary of prudent man.

The opposition of *thymos* and *bouleumata*, of passion and
reason, may very well have been invented in order to describe
Medea's peculiar situation: As a barbarian woman she is,
according to the Greeks, more prone to passion; there are no
social ties left that connect her with her new abode and that
now might restrain her. In favor of this assumption one may
adduce that Medea's monologue culminates in this distinction,
and this monologue is the gist of the whole drama. But here we
cannot be too sure. At any rate we shall find that Phaedra in
Euripides' second *Hippolytos* uses this distinction more freely
and in a more developed form.

The first two lines of Medea we quoted could have been
spoken by Phaedra some years earlier: "I am overcome by evil
and I realize what evil I am about to do." But the second two
fit only Medea, "My *thymos* is stronger than my resolution,
that *thymos* which is to blame for the greatest evils that men
commit." Medea expresses this conflict between passion and
clear-headed deliberation because she is bent on deed and plan,
because to a much greater degree than Phaedra she wants to
wreak vengeance on her husband. With her, the *thymos* is not
only the "incitement" but the passion which incites emotions,
because she knows this passion as the origin of the greatest
sufferings and of her future deeds. Medea knows *before* she acts
that what she is driven to do is bad, whereas Homer's men and
women are taught insight by experience. When the *thymos* has
done its work, "the fool recognizes what has been done."[9]
Aeschylus knows that action necessarily leads to suffering and

---

[9] *Il.* 17, 32 = 20, 198 ῥεχθὲν δέ τε νήπιος ἔγνω. Hes. *Opp.* 218 παθὼν δέ τε νήπιος ἔγνω.
Cf. *Philol. Unters.*, 29, 1924, 27, n. 3; F. Krafft, "Vergleichende Untersuchungen zu
Homer und Hesiod," *Hypomnemata*, 1963, p. 123.

therefore to recognition (δράσαντι παθεῖν, πάθει μάθος); Sophocles develops further this thought that all action is fundamentally unsafe and dangerous. The men in Aeschylus and Sophocles who are to be taken seriously are intent on doing what is right even if before acting they are aware of the problems involved in a decision. Medea takes in such considerations before acting—she knows from the outset that her deed is evil, but does it nevertheless.

Here, for the first time, a human being is so completely on his own that the only motive he knows for his action is his passion and his reflection. The inner impulse which drives Medea forward is the rebellion of the heart against a deep injury which Jason has done her. Her passion, which springs from just indignation, is elemental in its dimensions and can be sure of our fullest sympathy however horrible the deed may be that results from it.

Three years later, Euripides takes up these thoughts on the relationship between passion and reflection once again, in the second *Hippolytos*. There, Phaedra says in her monologue (380 ff.):

> τὰ χρήστ' ἐπιστάμεσθα καὶ γιγνώσκομεν
> οὐκ ἐκπονοῦμεν δ', οἳ μὲν ἀργίας ὕπο,
> οἳ δ' ἡδονὴν προθέντες ἀντὶ τοῦ καλοῦ
> ἄλλην τιν[ά].

"We know and recognize what is right [decent, good], but we do not do it; some out of laziness, others because they prefer some other pleasure to what is noble."

Phaedra conceives the problem in more general terms than Medea who spoke only of herself: "*I* know what evil *I* am about to do, but *my* thymos is stronger than *my* resolution." Phaedra, however, uses the first person plural: "*We* know[10] what is good but *we* do not do it," and she adds a lengthy discussion on how various pleasures seduce men.

---

[10] On the combination ἐπιστάμεσθα and γιγνώσκομεν see *Philol. Suppl.*, 20, 1, p. 18, n. 42.

Medea's considerations spring directly from her particular position and reproduce the quintessence of her action in the decisive situation. Phaedra's assertions stand in a more mediate relationship to her fate and the action of the tragedy—not alone because they do not form a summary of a hypercritical situation but rather a general introduction to a lengthy speech in which only gradually does she point out how she has tried to come to terms with her love; this reasoning bears only loosely on what has really befallen her. Before, her love for Hippolytos is described as a sickness, and this sickness has little to do with indolence (ἀργία) or with some kind of pleasure (ἡδονή), with garrulity (λέσχαι) or leisure (σχολή) which are mentioned in connection with the lines quoted,[11] and a few lines later, she returns (393) to the motive of sickness. These reflections (373–390) add nothing essential to the action of the drama or even to the purpose of the speech. Why Euripides included them is shown by the words quoted above (375 ff.): "I have wondered for many a long night what it is that destroys the life of men, and I do not believe that it is the nature of their knowledge that makes them do wrong,

καί μοι δοκοῦσιν οὐ κατὰ γνώμης φύσιν
πράσσειν κακίον(α).[12]

For many people possess right thinking (εὖ φρονεῖν). One must rather see the matter as follows"—and then follow the decisive lines already quoted: "We know what is good but do not do it, out of indolence and all kinds of inclination." Euripides is, therefore, anxious to set his point of view off against another opinion. Phaedra says she does not believe the opinion: that men do not εὖ πράσσειν, that they do not act as they should is due to φύσις γνώμης, to the constitution of their understanding and knowledge. We can see how this objection against which Euripides is defending himself fits Medea's monologue. Medea

---

[11] This becomes particularly clear when one tries, as Wilamowitz, for example, has done, to interpret these words "psychologically." Here more correctly M. Pohlenz, *Griech. Trag. Erl.*, p. 77 and K. Reinhardt, *Tradition und Geist*, p. 236

[12] κάκιον mss., κακίον' Cyrill., S. Schmid, Barrett.

had said: "I know that I am about to do the wrong thing
[κακῶς πράττειν] [καὶ μανθάνω μὲν οἷα δρᾶν μέλλω κακά], but
my passion [θυμός] is stronger than my considerations
[βουλεύματα]." Somebody then responds: "If the nature of
one's insight and knowledge [φύσις γνώμης][13] is in order, the
right kind of thinking, the εὖ φρονεῖν, will produce the right
kind of action [εὖ πράττειν]. One must therefore make sure
one has the right knowledge." In the second *Hippolytos*, however, Phaedra says: "Knowledge of what is right have many.
We know what is good but do not do it because we are at the
mercy of our ἡδοναί [desires]." Without going into the question
of what the right thing is, she answers: "Life is, however,
different; knowledge is no help at all, as Man lets himself be led
by other things." She restricts herself to the diagnosis and
considers the therapy dubious. This does not mean, however,
that Phaedra has not tried everything within her power to cure
herself of her sickness. She describes in detail her efforts to
master her passion. Adopting first of all the image of sickness
from the first *Hippolytos*, she then enlarges upon Medea's
metaphor of the inner struggle (388 ff.):

When I considered this, there was no remedy[14] to dispose of it so
that I might come to another conviction. I shall relate to you the
course of my understanding; when I was wounded by love, I pondered
on how I might most honourably conduct myself. I began by conceal-
ing the sickness, by keeping it a secret . . . The second course I
took was to bear this foolishness with decorum by overcoming it by
self-possession [ἄνοιαν . . . τῷ σωφρονεῖν νικῶσα]. As I did not succeed
in mastering Aphrodite [Κύπριν κρατῆσαι], my third course was to
take my own life. The disgrace must remain a secret; it is the only
way to preserve my good reputation.

One cannot say, therefore, that she let herself drift venially.
In the first *Hippolytos* the nurse had been the warner and had

---

[13] Barrett seems to me too vague in his translation "bent of men's minds," and if
he maintains that γνώμη is "the mind as seat of moral dispositions." By the following
εὖ φρονεῖν and particularly by ἐπιστάμεσθα καὶ γιγνώσκομεν she makes quite clear that
she means the intellectual power.

[14] Like Archilochos, she says φάρμακον.

tried to free Phaedra from her passion. Now Phaedra herself makes every honest effort to emerge victorious from the inner battle. It is no longer a conflict between two different persons, but a conflict within the soul of a single person, the battle of wisdom against passion and folly.

The nurse in this drama is again the *confidante* of Phaedra, but this time she has a different task: she thwarts Phaedra's suicide plan by expressing her willingness to take over the role of mediator, and fate runs its course.

Who, then, raised objection to Medea's reflections and said: "Knowledge of what is right leads to the right course of action"? To whom is Phaedra here replying? To ask the question amounts to as much as answering it. We are acquainted with this point of view from Plato's early dialogues, but in Xenophon Socrates[15] too speaks like this: "When asked whether he believed that those men were wise and weak who know what had to be done but nevertheless did the opposite, he answered: Rather are they unwise and weak, for I believe that all those who choose from possibilities do what appears most to their advantage."[16] For these words of Socrates, directed against the assertion that a man could have insight and yet lack self-control, we need only presuppose Euripides' Medea who knows so exactly where her path is leading her. The idea, to be sure, undergoes a small but significant shift of emphasis. Medea

---

[15] Th. Barthold in his edition of *Hippolytos* (1880, p. 39, on line 380) correctly interpreted Phaedra's lines as a polemic against Socrates, as H. Hommel, *Epigraphica*, 19, 1959, 144, n. 2, reminds me. Cf. also Wilamowitz, *Hermes*, 15, 1880, 516 = *Kl. Schr.* 1, 51 f.; and *Einl. in d. gr. Trag.*, p. 25, n. 44; Decharme, *Euripide et l'esprit de son théâtre*, pp. 46 f.; Dodds, *The Greeks and the Irrational*, pp. 186 and 199, nn. 47 and 49; R. P. Winnington-Ingram, *Entretiens Hardt* 6, 1958, 174. W. S. Barrett in his commentary to Eur. Hipp., 377–381, objects strongly to the opinion that Socrates has anything to do with the words of Phaedra. See below, p. 6of.

[16] Xenophon *Memor.* 3, 9, 4: προσερωτώμενος δὲ εἰ τοὺς ἐπισταμένους μὲν ἃ δεῖ πράττειν, ποιοῦντας δὲ τἀναντία, σοφούς τε καὶ ἀκρατεῖς εἶναι νομίζοι. οὐδὲν γε μᾶλλον, ἔφη, ἢ ἀσόφους τε καὶ ἀκρατεῖς· πάντας γὰρ οἶμαι προαιρομένους ἐκ τῶν ἐνδεχομένων ἃ οἴονται συμφορώτερα αὐτοῖς εἶναι, ταῦτα πράττειν. Apparently ἀκρατής, "weak," refers to a person who, like Medea, was not strong enough to win the inner struggle. This "moral" meaning of ἀκρατής (as well as that of ἐγκρατής) does not occur before Medea has said that her thymos is stronger than her βουλεύματα.

said she realized what evil she was about to do, whereas Socrates is asked whether the man is wise who knows what should be done but does not do it. The knowledge of what is evil, therefore, is replaced by the knowledge of what is right. Here the view is diverted from the individual situation in which a man is at the mercy of disaster toward a general validity which helps one to come to terms with evil. And this is where Phaedra joins in: We know what is the correct thing to do, the decent, the good (τὰ χρηστά), but we do not do it.

We hear Socrates continuing the discussion beyond *Hippolytos* when he attacks Phaedra's words. In Plato's dialogue, he says to Protagoras:

"You know that most people do not believe you and me [that knowledge has the upper hand in man][17] but maintain that many recognize what is best but are not prepared to do it even if they could."[18] Socrates goes on: "As many as I have asked [there must therefore have been some discussion on the subject] why that is, have said that those who acted thus did so because they were overcome by desire [ἡδονῆς ἡττουμένους] or suffering [λύπης]."

Beforehand (352 B) he had named *thymos* as Euripides in *Medea* (1079), ἡδονή as Euripides in *Hippolytos* (382), λύπη, ἔρως as Phaedra had done, and φόβος. But these similar concepts are not so important. We have seen that this concept of an inner struggle, of a battle between reason and passion, was evidently first indicated by Euripides in *Medea* and first clearly formulated in *Hippolytos* II. It is this which Socrates takes up here.

Barrett in his commentary on Euripides' *Hippolytos* (p. 229) says, Phaedra "is polemizing not against the Socratic explaining away of moral weakness in terms of ignorance but against the

[17] σοφίαν καὶ ἐπιστήμην . . . πάντων κράτιστον . . . εἶναι τῶν ἀνθρωπείων πραγμάτων.
[18] Plato, *Prot.* 352 D: οἶσθα οὖν ὅτι οἱ πολλοὶ τῶν ἀνθρώπων ἐμοί τε καὶ σοὶ οὐ πείθονται, ἀλλὰ πολλούς φασι γιγνώσκοντας τὰ βέλτιστα οὐκ ἐθέλειν πράττειν, ἐξὸν αὐτοῖς, ἀλλὰ ἄλλα πράττειν. That these words refer to Phaedra, cf. Wilamowitz, *Einl., op. cit.*; *Hippolytos*, pp. 203 f.; Nestle, *Euripides*, pp. 473 f. and 495, and in his Protagoras commentary on the passage p. 134; Schadewaldt, *Monolog*, p. 110, n. 2. Dodds, *op. cit.*, is sceptical on this point.

much simpler view that wrong-doing is ordinarily due to natural vice." Is that indeed the simpler view for Greeks of the fifth century? I am afraid, Barrett has here taken Christian thoughts as natural and as existing at all times. To be sure, somebody in the *Hippolytos* has said (fr. 444):

> ὦ δαῖμον, ὡς οὐκ ἔστ᾽ ἀποστροφὴ βροτοῖς
> τῶν ἐμφύτων τε καὶ θεηλάτων κακῶν,

"O daemon, that there is no escape for man from the inborn and from the god-sent evils," and later in his Bellerophontes (fr. 297) Euripides speaks of ἔμφυτος πᾶσιν ἀνθρώποις κάκη (see below, p. 65), but for the earlier times I see only two ways in which one could look upon the psychological origin of wrong-doing: either man is blind (we shall come back to that) and has a violent *thymos*—that is the Homeric and archaic way[19]— or he is weak. This is, as we have seen, something new in Euripides' Admetus and in the first Phaedra and is developed further to an "inner conflict" in *Medea*, but vice, sin, inborn evil are not yet brought into consideration. Phaedra subsumes all irrational motives that are stronger than reason under the heading "pleasures," ἡδοναί.[20]

About Socrates' words in Plato's *Protagoras*—"most people know what is good but are not ready to do it"—Barrett says: "When Plato cites this as the ordinary man's opinion there is no earthly reason why he should be thought to refer to one particular exponent." But Plato says clearly that when he

---

[19] For Bacchylides it is desire of gain, love, and ambition that prevent men from leading a pious life; cf. C. M. Bowra, *Hermes* 91, 1963, 257 ff.

[20] Phaedra 381 says οὐκ ἐκπονοῦμεν δ᾽ οἱ μὲν ἀργίας ὕπο, οἱ δ᾽ ἡδονὴν προθέντες ἀντὶ τοῦ καλοῦ ἄλλην τιν᾽, εἰσὶ δ᾽ ἡδοναὶ πολλαὶ βίου and she enumerates as "pleasures" λέσχαι, σχολή, αἰδώς. ἀργία is laziness that we do not "bring to completion by means of πόνος" (as Barrett circumscribes ἐκπονοῦμεν, 381) what we have recognized as right. The "pleasures" correspond to the ἄνοια in 398 in her "inner struggle". It is apparent, I should say, that she accommodates her personal situation to the scheme developed by Medea: θυμὸς κρείσσων τῶν βουλευμάτων. But since Medea does not speak of pleasure and since it is not the most natural thing to bring in here λέσχαι, σχολή, αἰδώς as "pleasures" it seems possible that Phaedra uses words brought forward by Socrates in his polemics against Medea—and indeed Socrates in Plato's Protagoras speaks of ἡδοναί in a much more appropriate context.

asks people about this, they speak of inner conflict (ἡδονῆς ἡττουμένους, etc.)—but that is Euripides, and when Barrett quotes examples for these convictions, he quotes—Euripides.[21] At the time of Plato's *Protagoras* they may very well have been common—Plato considers such moral indolence as simply plebeian and vulgar, and refutes Phaedra's words that "many" people have insight.

But let us suppose for a moment that the Socrates of the Platonic *Protagoras* is not expressing the thoughts of the historical Socrates. That would cause considerable difficulties. Objections were raised against Euripides' Medea, and their main point was to interpret knowledge and correct action from the strictly moral point of view. These objections are taken up by the Phaedra of the second *Hippolytos*. It is true that Socrates and Protagoras in Plato's dialogue are agreed that knowledge determines virtue. As a teacher of virtue, Protagoras believes in its teachability; nevertheless the assertion which Phaedra answers so zealously and urgently cannot come from Protagoras, for example. For although his wish is to educate men to healthy deliberation (εὐβουλία), what is right (τὰ χρηστὰ) is not for him, on principle, in opposition to pleasure (ἡδονή) as Phaedra's speech presupposes. One might, on a fleeting reading of Phaedra's words, interpret the πράττειν κακίον(α) as "bad condition," especially when one takes the manuscripts' reading κάκιον. But here Barrett is right in stating that the meaning "do wrong" is required. If we take πράττειν κάκιον as "fare badly," the following words could possibly be interpreted as a polemic against Protagoras: "In my view, it is not the fault of knowledge that things go badly for men, for many possess insight. No, this is how we must see it: we know what is good but do not do it because we permit ourselves to be led by indolence and pleasure." The objection raised against Medea would then merely have meant: when one is sensible, such things cannot happen. But for Phaedra, her unhappy love for her stepson is a moral phenomenon, not

---

[21] I shall come back to these quotations on p. 63ff.

merely a question of her well-being. Therefore, her reflections on knowledge would lose all meaning if the κακῶς πράττειν and the χρηστόν were not taken ethically in the strictest sense; but as the moral concept of εὖ πράττειν appears here in the objection which Phaedra criticizes, it cannot have been Protagoras but Socrates who raised the objection. And if anyone would like to suggest that we do not know enough about the details of the discussions carried on in the Athens of the time to be able to ascribe with certainty such a disconnected sentence to its author, that would mean more or less that the main tenet of Socratic philosophy did not come from Socrates. This does not imply, however, that these problems did not remain topical, that they were not discussed animatedly up to and beyond the time of Plato's Protagoras.[22]

As philologists, we educate ourselves to taking each word exactly, pedantically; and with good writers—but only with good ones—it pays dividends. For a writer is a good writer when he takes his words seriously. In Euripides and Plato, we presuppose that they knew what they were saying, and an interpretation that waters down their words has little or no plausibility. But once we recognize that Euripides as well as Socrates brings forward new ideas the reciprocal arguments fit perfectly together.

That Euripides in *Hippolytos* is engaged in a dispute with Socrates is proved conclusively by the fact that he takes the matter up again later. We have two fragments from his *Chrysippus*, both of which speak of the moral impotence of knowledge. Laios who appears here evidently as the "inventor" of paederasty, says (fr. 840): "Nothing of what you reproach

---

[22] This remains chiefly for the Stoa precisely the fundamental moral problem and since St. Paul Christians have been tackling it. W. Nestle in his commentary to Plat. *Prot.* 352 D quotes several passages. The metaphor of the inner battle is used by Democritus, that is before Plato (65 B 214), "Not he alone is bold who conquers his enemies but also he who overcomes his pleasures" (ἀνδρεῖος οὐχ ὁ τῶν πολεμίων μόνον, ἀλλὰ καὶ ὁ τῶν ἡδονῶν κρείσσων). However uncertain Democritus' dates may be, it is improbable that he spoke this sentence before 431, i.e., before the performance of Medea.

me with is a secret to me; but even if I have insight, I am compelled by nature, by constitution":

λέληθεν οὐδὲν τῶνδέ μ'ὧν σὺ νουθετεῖς·
γνώμην δ'ἔχοντά μ' ἡ φύσις βιάζεται.

Apparently, Chrysippus, his "lover," replies (fr. 841): "Alas, that is an evil imposed on men by the gods when someone knows good but does not make use of his knowledge":

αἰαῖ, τόδ' ἤδη θεῖον ἀνθρώποις κακόν,
ὅταν τις εἰδῇ τἀγαθόν, χρῆται δὲ μή.

In the meantime these problems are well known, they have lost their exciting novelty, Laios is prepared for such a discussion. More important is that this exchange accentuates the philosophical element in the contrast between nature (φύσις) and insight (γνώμη) much more strongly than before.[23] It can also be sophistic, but when Chrysippus no longer speaks in the plural of the "evil things," the κακά, as Medea, nor of the "good things," the χρηστά, as Phaedra, but instead uses the expression εἰδέναι τὸ ἀγαθόν, "to know the good," that is certainly Socratic. True, that does not presuppose that "the good" was already being brought into play as an object of research, as a subject of philosophical speculation, or even as the idea of the good. What both sides, Euripides and Socrates, understand by "the good" is something relatively simple: it is a general idea to which one can immediately appeal, something which makes a discussion possible.

About the year 410 B.C., Euripides formulated the inner conflict once again in sharp antitheses, in the fr. 220 of his *Antiope*, "many mortals endure this evil: filled with reasonable insight, they nevertheless do not wish to subject themselves to the soul, because they are for the most part defeated by what is dear and pleasing to them":

---

[23] Cf. γνώμης φύσις in *Hipp.* 377; on the other hand in Aristoph. *Nub.* 1078 the Ἄδικος Λόγος says: "χρῶ τῇ φύσει, σκίρτα, γέλα, νόμιζε μηδὲν αἰσχρόν." Both these passages do not contain the notion of "conflict," though in Aristophanes φύσις is already opposed to σωφρονεῖν (1071) and Zeus ἥττων ἔρωτός ἐστιν (1081).

πολλοὶ δὲ θνητῶν τοῦτο πάσχουσιν κακόν.
γνώμῃ φρονοῦντες οὐ θέλουσ' ὑπηρετεῖν
ψυχῇ τὰ πολλὰ πρὸς φίλων νικώμενοι.

Here, it is worth noting that the "soul," the ψυχή, is on the side of insight (γνώμη) and reason (φρόνησις), in contrast to what one desires (φίλα). It appears that this is the first instance in which the "soul" has this meaning, and this presupposes surely that the conflict between desire and insight is seen as a conflict between body and soul. This is also Socratic. Once again, Euripides says that many men are like this—he does not say it high-mindedly and disparagingly as does Socrates for whom it is simply below his dignity, but rather submissively, as an established fact. We have seen (p. 61) that Euripides in the first *Hippolytos* and in *Bellerophontes* speaks of the inborn and god sent κακά and says that the bad (evil, vile) is implanted in the nature of all men, ὡς ἔμφυτος μὲν πᾶσιν ἀνθρώποις κάκη,[24] whereas Socrates cannot get away from the thought that there is good in all men from birth and that man can recognize and follow it. Euripides does not share this optimism—and many have since gone along with him:

> Vainement ma raison voulait prendre la barre;
> La tempête en jouant déroutait ses efforts.
> (Baudelaire, *Les sept vieillards*)

If we suppose that Socrates taught "virtue is knowledge" and "if men do not act correctly, it is because they do not think correctly" as early as 428 B.C., and that Euripides is attacking him for it in *Hippolytos*,[25] then there is a further

---

[24] Cf. also fr. 572 from the *Oinomaos* (ca. 408 B.C.): ἀλλὰ ταῦτα γὰρ λέγειν ἐπιστάμεσθα, δρᾶν δ' ἀμηχάνως ἔχει, and the lines quoted in *Pap. Soc. It.*, 4, 280 (Nauck³ fr. ad.323 b), "He who believes that thought (φρόνησις) is the way to happiness is a fool. For life is governed not by insight but by chance." Both sense and metrical form show that this is not pre-Euripides.

[25] I do not consider it necessary to establish any influence of Socrates in further passages of *Hippolytos*. When, for example, the nurse says (358), "οἱ σώφρονες γὰρ οὐχ ἑκόντες ἀλλ' ὅμως κακῶν ἐρῶσι," we do not have to read the sentence of Socrates οὐδεὶς ἑκὼν ἁμαρτάνει behind it, for with σώφρονες are meant not those who know on account of philosophical education, but the chaste, the self-controlled: even they can

question to be looked into: is it possible that Socrates by contradicting the sentence spoken by Medea "my *thymos* is stronger than my sound considerations" first arrived at the cardinal tenet of his teaching? No doubt, Socrates' opinion that virtue is knowledge picks up several threads from older points of view: "knowledge" had indeed already been a determining factor for correct action in the ethics of the early Greeks. But this implied merely that one must understand a work in order to do it properly (ἐπίστασθαι, σοφός, τέχνη imply this kind of knowledge) or that one must be sober and keep his eyes open in order not to stumble into disaster (that means to be σώφρων, to beware of *hubris*; the Delphic sentences γνῶθι σεαυτόν, μηδὲν ἄγαν aim at this). But the fundamental and radical element of the idea, to judge from the way in which all other new things came into the world, certainly did not originate without a thesis to which there was an antithesis. And, indeed, we need search no further than this line from *Medea* to explain the antithesis of Socrates. Then we should be able to date the origin of this important thought exactly. However that may be, we nevertheless find Socrates here in opposition to Euripides—or, to be more exact, to words uttered by characters in Euripidean plays[26]—not, however, in opposition to the sophists. For when dealing with the sophists, Socrates does not need to emphasize the importance of knowledge for action (in the same way as Socrates in the passage already quoted from Plato's Protagoras can represent himself and the sophist as being of the same opinion). The contrast to the sophists lies rather in the fact that Socrates takes knowledge seriously as "real" knowledge and that he dismisses the knowledge of the sophists as sham knowledge—and it is uncertain

---

be seduced by Aphrodite. On the contrary, it is the other way round: Socrates' sentence presupposes such assertions as the Nurse makes. Line 79 ὅστις διδακτὸν μηδέν, ἀλλ' ἐν τῇ φύσει τὸ σωφρονεῖν εἴληχεν, is also spoken without "philosophy" (cf. Schadewaldt, Monolog, p. 111, n. 2). For another influence of Socrates on Eur., cf. Christ-Schmid, *Gesch. d. griech. Lit.*, I, 3, 1, p. 275, n. 2.

[26] Barrett rightly stresses this point (p. 229). But it is Euripides who has laid bare these problems, and so they must have been his own concern.

when this Parmenidean motif of separating semblance from reality became significant for Socrates' ethical speculations. At any rate, Socrates must have arrived at the fundamental observation that virtue is knowledge before he could claim that this knowledge had to be genuine and not sham. And so it would be possible for Socrates to have arrived at the assertion that virtue was knowledge through Euripides' *Medea*, and that the quarrel with the sophists, that is to say, the battle against sham knowledge and the search for firm knowledge on virtue —these significant preoccupations of Socrates—occurred at a later date. This naturally does not mean that Socrates had not occupied himself earlier with a variety of philosophical questions but merely that the essential part of his philosophizing did not take place until late. This is only one way of imagining Socrates' development but it is confirmed from two quarters: In the *Clouds* by Aristophanes, which was performed in 423 B.C., five years after *Hippolytos*, we sense nowhere that Socrates is an opponent of the Sophists. This has led to people not giving credence to Aristophanes' portrayal, which is certainly the wrong thing to do. Secondly, the battle with the sophists and all the sober and philosophical elements connected with it were the ardent preoccupation of the Socrates whom his pupils knew in the last years of his life. Are we to imagine then that Socrates, a man who never gave up his searches and enquiries, kept on thinking the one thought during the last thirty years of his life? That despite his ever lively passion for asking questions no new questions occurred to him for decades?

Finally, this discussion between Euripides and Socrates, who was ten years his junior, illuminates dazzlingly the turn which Attic thinking takes with Socrates: Euripides brings the passions into play as they are in human life. Phaedra only wonders what it is that disrupts human life at its foundations (376: ᾗ διέφθαρται βίος). Socrates, however, demands knowledge in order to remove the evil. Works of poetry can be written from Euripides' point of view—but Socrates' interjection strikes the very marrow of tragedy. In the face of his "philosophical" interest, tragic conflicts become irrelevant; the decent man in his opinion comes to terms with the difficulties of his nature in a sober, unpathetic manner by striving to recognize what is good, and then simply by doing it.

The *Achilleis* of Aeschylus taught us better to understand the transition from shame culture to guilt culture. The lost first *Hippolytos* revealed how a psychological interpretation of human action breaks up the mythological concepts on the one hand, and on the other hand shifts the values of right. The second *Hippolytos* shows us how philosophy takes up questions which had previously been treated by poets, and how art must therewith step into the background.

So far, I have not touched upon one feature of the second *Hippolytos*, namely that the goddesses Aphrodite and Artemis are of great importance for the action of the drama. It might seem that Euripides simply returns to the old mythological motivation of human actions, if he explains the disaster befalling the house of Theseus—Phaedra and Hippolytos—as the work of Aphrodite. In fact Aphrodite in the prologue says that she is going to take revenge on Hippolytos this very day (21), because he leads a chaste life (13 f.), is following Artemis, and does not give her, the Goddess of Love, due honor (τιμή), calling her the worst of all gods (13). Therefore she has caused Phaedra to love her stepson passionately (28) and she gives a short account of what we are going to experience on the stage.

Therewith we seem to be taken back to Homer, where, so to speak on the higher stage of Olympus, the decisions are made about the actions and the fate of mortals.

But the difference is that Euripides gives a full psychological explanation of Phaedra's love and of her actions during the drama. Therefore the participation of the goddess is much less necessary than in Homer, and Euripides has introduced the conflict of Aphrodite and Artemis not so much in order to make us understand *Phaedra* but in order to make us feel that the conflict of this drama is more than the fortuitous controversy of any person at all, but the clash of vital human tendencies.

The goddesses become symbols[27] of different ways of life, of different *bioi*. The psychological motivation fills us with immediate sympathy for our fellow mortals, the divine background allows us to feel the necessity and dignity of what we experience.

Phaedra herself does not look at the goddess who has led her into misfortune in the same way as the Homeric heroes who, having done something wrong, could say: not I am guilty but the god who has blinded me. She feels that the moral blame is upon her. And different, too, is her attitude to the old values of shame, honor, and *sophrosyne*. Phaedra—and Medea before her, and, in fact, even Achilles in Aeschylus' drama—seem to say: it is all very well for man to keep up his reputation, and of course it is nice to be wise and to constrain oneself—but that has become rather a platitude, it does not cover my situation; one must take into more serious account something else, that alone gives value to an individual.

Euripides shows this by associating Phaedra with Aphrodite and Hippolytos with Artemis: Their different lives are not merely personal moods or hobbies, but rather the necessary differences that appear wherever life creates certain forms.

Certainly Euripides in his second *Hippolytos* has made Phaedra more εὐκλεής, more honorable, less vicious, by letting her feel and act under the command of Aphrodite. But he has not weakened her passion nor softened the disaster by which the whole family is destroyed. He *has* shown that her personal fate is deeply rooted in nature, and by introducing the goddesses he has made her all the more human.

But since Xenophanes it had become obvious that the Greek gods were of little real help for moral embarrassments, and so it is no wonder that in the second *Hippolytos* we find Euripides engaged in philosophical discussion.

---

[27] Important steps toward a "symbolic" interpretation of the Olympian gods had been taken, i.e., by Empedocles (fr. 6 D.) and Sophocles (fr. 361 P.).

IV

Vita Activa and
Vita Contemplativa in
Euripides' *Antiope*

ANTIOPE WAS one of the last tragedies Euripides brought to the Athenian stage, about twenty years after the second *Hippolytos*. In spite of this long interval, some of the motifs of the older dramas turn up again here, in particular the question of shaping the *bios*, the way of life, and the problem of how much man can achieve by his intellectual powers. Euripides in *Antiope* raises these problems to a highly abstract level by introducing two brothers who represent two different ways of life: one of them adheres to the *vita activa*, the other to the *vita contemplativa*. The discussion in which each defends his own ideal was a famous piece of rhetoric, and it is especially this part that will interest us. Unfortunately, the drama itself is lost, but we have a number of quotations and allusions and a fragment on a piece of papyrus. The discussion between the two brothers was used by Plato in his *Gorgias*— though there the Euripidean verses are not quoted in a context concerned with the practical and theoretical life, but with might and right, a theme Euripides treated in the *Phoenissae*, that is, at a time not far off from his *Antiope*.

But before I turn to this dialogue, I would like to sketch the action of the drama as far as we can reconstruct it from the fragments[1]—it will be seen that Euripides balanced the high-brow conversation of the brothers with a thrilling plot.

The stage is laid, as we now know from a recently deciphered passage in a manuscript of Strabo,[2] in Eleutherae, a small Attic place at the Mountain Cythaeron on the border of Boeotia, where an old cult of Dionysus was observed. In fact from here the cult of Dionysus Eleutherius had been transferred by Peisistratos to Athens. In this region Antiope, the daughter of Nykteus, king of Thebes, had borne two children by Zeus. She had to flee before the wrath of her father (who had the speaking name "Night man") and had given the boys whom she called Zethos and Amphion[3] to a shepherd, a slave

---

[1] The fundamental work on the *Antiope* still is Hans Schaal, *De Euripidis Antiopa*, a Berlin dissertation of 1914 supervised by Wilamowitz and Loeschcke. Wherever Schaal's arguments have convinced me, I have taken over his results without discussion. There are only minor points where I differ from him, and they mostly concern passages that he has attributed to a certain context without looking sharply enough at the wording. A closer examination usually proves that Schaal was right, but that his arguments can be strengthened, and sometimes the context can be made out more clearly. But of course in such investigations some uncertainty always remains. T. B. L. Webster (*The Classic. Trad.*, . . . *Studies in Honor of H. Caplan*, N.Y., 1966, 83f.) suggests that *Hypsipyle*, *Phoenissae*, and *Antiope* belonged to the same trilogy of the year 410 B.C. This is very tempting, but then one should expect the order *Antiope*, *Hypsipyle*, *Phoenissae*. Recently U. Hausmann, *Ath. Mitt.*, 73, 1958 (1962), 50–72, has published a "Homeric cup" in whose illustrations he sees scenes of Euripides' *Antiope*.

[2] Cod. V according to W. Aly, cf. Aly-Sbordone, "De Strab. cod. rescr.," *Studi e Testi* 188, pp. 16 and 281, Città del Vatic. 1956. Fr. 179 now reads (Strab. 8, 6, 16 p. 375):

ἔχειν

σύ μοι διδοίης δεσπότῃ θ' ὃς Οἰνόης
σύγχορτα ναίει πεδία ταῖσδ' Ἐλευθεραῖς.

1 before ἔχειν one expects something like εὐπραξίαν or rather, because Strabo would scarcely have omitted such a noun, a relative clause as ἃ . . . εὐχόμεσθ' or the like ‖ **2** σύ seems to be Dionysos | οἰνόης *V*, οἰνώνη cett. | δεσπότῃ sc. Οἰνεῖ, cf. Dion Chrys. 15, 9 (2, 234 Arn.) ‖ **3** ναίει Strab. V, ναίειν cett., ναίω *Schol.* AT ad *Il.* 11, 774.

This ms. has decided, too, the much discussed question of who spoke the prologue: it was the shepherd (so rightly Wecklein, Graf, Arnim, Schaal), see below, p. 72.

[3] It is uncertain whether we have to read κικλήσκω (with Wecklein) in fr. 181 or κίκλησκε with the mss. (or rather κικλήσκει with Valckenaer, since the form without augment is not very welcome). Hyg. 8 and Apollod. 3, 5, 5 say, Antiope gave the name to Zethos, and in fact it seems more probable that Antiope called the boy Zethos because ἐζήτησε . . . τόκοισιν εὐμάρειαν ἡ τεκοῦσά νιν, and not the shepherd after hearing

of Oineus,[4] who lived in a modest hut in Eleutherai. There he brought up the boys as shepherds. In the meantime Antiope married King Epopeus of Sikyon. Nykteus before his death ordered his brother Lykos to punish Antiope for her disgrace. Lykos conquers Sikyon, kills Epopeus, brings Antiope, in fetters, home to Thebes, and delivers her for punishment to his cruel wife Dirke. But in a miraculous way Antiope is freed from her fetters—they dissolve "automatically," as Apollodorus (3, 5, 5) says, thanks probably to Zeus. She flees and arrives at the hut of the shepherd where her sons live now grown to manhood.

Euripides' play begins shortly before her arrival. In the prologue the shepherd reports the events of the past. To this part of the drama belong the verses quoted by Strabo which, as mentioned, make it certain that the scene was laid in Eleutherai and that the shepherd spoke the prologue. The prologue can be further reconstructed: The play *Antiope* by the early Roman dramatist Pacuvius apparently was a translation or at least a close adaption of the Euripidean play to the Roman stage, hence fragments of his prologue will be useful for us. We shall see later that we can gain even more from Pacuvius for the reconstruction of Euripides' *Antiope*. The verse from the prologue is (347 R.): *exorto iubare, noctis decurso itinere*, "Since the sun[5] has risen after having accomplished his nocturnal way." This shows that it is early morning, and often in the beginning of a Greek drama the rising sun is greeted in

the story from Antiope as Schaal supposes. But Schaal is certainly right (and this is much more important) that the shepherd got the boys from Antiope and heard from her that the boys were of royal descent and that the mother exposed them because she had been disgraced by having these children. About a certain difficulty arising from this assumption see p. 75, n. 14.

[4] That he is a slave appears from the word δεσπότῃ fr. 179, 2.

[5] Varro *op. cit.* 6, 6 says that *iubar* here was the sun. He further says that a *pastor* said these words. Since we now know for certain that the shepherd spoke the prologue, the assumption is strongly confirmed that this verse belongs to the Antiope and to its prologue. If this prologue began with a prayer to Dionysus it is possible that the hut of the shepherd was somehow connected with a sanctuary of Dionysus and that this was the cave where Zeus approached Antiope as a satyr (cf. Hausmann, *op. cit.*, p. 70).

this way.[6] Wilamowitz[7] supplements these words by *surgo ad operas meas* ("I get up to do my work"). But since the shepherd must have gone on to tell how the two boys came to him, he most likely had a special reason for recalling this old story. And since he prays to Dionysos to give [welfare?] to him and to his master he seems to be worried. A frequent motivation in such cases is a dream and perhaps it was here too. The shepherd goes away for some time so that he is not present in the following scenes.

Amphion enters the stage and attracts the chorus of old Athenians by a song (Schaal, p. 7). A singing shepherd is familiar to us from Theokritos and Vergil, but, a long time before Euripides, Stesichoros introduced the shepherd Daphnis as a musician. Ordinarily shepherds use a syrinx to accompany their songs, but Amphion has the solemn lyre (fr. 190), and he sings in Terpandrian dactyls.[8] He sings "philosophy" as far as that is possible for a mythical figure: a cosmogony about the elements. When Zethos enters the stage in order to go hunting,[9] he scolds at the lazy life of his brother, and so begins the famous discussion about the values of the active and the contemplative life to which we shall return later. For the moment I mention only that Euripides characterizes the two brothers as a kind of Hippolytos and Phaedra—the hunter and the "lazy" (ἀεργός) person.

Again Euripides uses an older pattern and gives it a new meaning. Former experience might make us expect that new ideas would be brought forward in this way. But that we shall discuss later. First I would like to go on with the narration of the action as far as we can recognize it.

At the end of the dialogue Amphion "cedes to the way of life of Zethos" as Horace puts it,[10] so that the brothers can act

---

[6] Cf. above p. 27.

[7] Ap. Schaal 6, n. 1.

[8] Cf. Soph., *Thamyras* fr. 221 N.² and Ps.-Terpand. Diehl V, p. 1 from Aristoxenos, fr. 84 W.

[9] Hor. *Ep.* 1, 18, 42 about Zethos: *cum venari velit;* cf. Hippolytos in Eur. *Hipp.* 58 ff.

[10] *Ep.* 1, 18, 41 ff. *fraternis cessisse putatur moribus Amphion.*

unanimously in the further course of the play. A mere technical reason caused Euripides to reconcile them: from now on Zethos apparently is a mute person: according to the conventions of the Attic theater never more than three persons taking part in a dialogue can be on the stage at the same time; at the end of the play Amphion and Zethos are present and two other characters. Amphion takes part in the conversation, Zethos does not. So Amphion has to speak for both, and that is only possible after a reconciliation.

Now Antiope enters. The chorus seems to ask her who she is and she answers (fr. 204):

$$πόλλ' ἔστιν ἀνθρώποισιν, ὦ ξένοι, κακά$$

"There is, O strangers, much misfortune". Supplementing the prologue of the shepherd, she relates that she bore two children (fr. 207) after Zeus had clandestinely approached her in the disguise of a satyr. Amphion responds that he could not believe Zeus would behave like a human being in this way.[11] With indignation Antiope answers (fr. 216):

$$οὐ χρή ποτ' ἄνδρα δοῦλον ὄντ' ἐλευθέρας$$
$$γνώμας διώκειν οὐδ' ἐς ἀργίαν βλέπειν$$

"A man who is a slave ought never to follow up convictions [reasonings, cognitions] of a free man and should not look at a lazy life."

She disapproves of his free speech as not befitting a slave and of his laziness—with this word possibly she aims at his σχολή and his sophisticated *éclairissement*, as shortly before Zethos had used the same word for his musical and theoretical interests. She speaks these insulting words to Amphion in her

---

[11] Fr. 207: Antiope: ἡνίκ' ἡγόμην πάλιν | κύουσ' ἔτικτον (Does πάλιν mean that she had been taken away by Zeus from her home and possibly kept somewhere for a certain time?). Fr. 210: Amphion: οὐδὲ γὰρ λάθρα δοκῶ | θηρὸς (sic F. K. Schmidt, φωτὸς ms.) κακούργου σχήματ' ἐκμιμούμενον | σοὶ Ζῆν' ἐς εὐνὴν ὥσπερ ἄνθρωπον μολεῖν. Perhaps Antiope first answers rather mildly with fr. 206 (cf. Wilamowitz ap. Schaal 18, 3; cf. p. 92, n. 49.).

pride as the daughter of a king and the lover of Zeus.[12] Another
fragment (fr. 218) may belong to this scene:

φεῦ, φεῦ, το δοῦλον ὡς ἀπανταχῇ γένος
πρὸς τὴν ἐλάσσω μοῖραν ὥρισεν θεός

and Amphion could have spoken them: "O, how god has everywhere destined the class of slaves to a lower fortune"—and
mean that once one is a slave one has to suffer insults from
above. But it is possible too that Antiope says these words, and
"everywhere" would be especially appropriate for her. With
these words Antiope, then, may very well allude to her own
experience as a slave too. Some fragments from Pacuvius show
that she herself spoke of the hardships she had to suffer as a
slave.[13] But then it is not clear whether she spoke these words
in the dialogue with Amphion or in a monologue, which, I
assume, followed this scene.[14]

Of course, the point of this dialogue between mother and son
is that they do not recognize one another and that each makes
erroneous reproaches to the other. Amphion does not know
that Antiope really has been loved by Zeus (nor has he the
slightest idea that he is their son) and Antiope does not know
that Amphion is not a slave, but her own child, the grandson
of Zeus. It is an irony of errors of which the old Euripides is so
fond.

Amphion, of course, is deeply offended by Antiope's words
that a slave should keep to thoughts corresponding to his low
social standing, especially since he must assume that Antiope

[12] Fr. 216 could also have been said by Zethos in his discussion with Amphion. Then
the words would mean: "We are both slaves, therefore we should limit ourselves to
practical work of humble people. We must not strive at the musical and intellectual
interests of the freeborn." But we have no sign of such resignation in the other fragments of Zethos' speech, and it would contradict the strength of his arguments that
are concentrated on the principles of life.

[13] Fr. 5–7 and 15 R.; cf. Prop. 3, 15, 15.

[14] There is one other difficulty in this scene: Antiope apparently flees to the region
where once she left her children. Why, then, does she not suspect that Amphion who is
the appropriate age is one of them?

herself is a slave or not much more and that by bragging she gives herself the air of having been loved by Zeus.

These words about slavery are not only general statements,[15] but precise contributions to a sharp dialogue. For the further course of the drama we need a scene where the two sons try to expel their mother again from the hut.[16] After this clash with his mother we understand Amphion's hostility, and it is only natural to assume that he rushes off to seek help from the old shepherd and his brother. So there is room for a monologue by Antiope, and indeed, the beginning of it seems to have been preserved (fr. 211):

$$\varphi\epsilon\hat{v}, \ \varphi\epsilon\hat{v} \ \beta\rho o\tau\epsilon\acute{\iota}\omega\nu \ \pi\eta\mu\acute{\alpha}\tau\omega\nu \ \~\delta\sigma\alpha\iota \ \tau\acute{v}\chi\alpha\iota$$
$$\~\delta\sigma\alpha\iota \ \tau\epsilon \ \mu o\rho\varphi\alpha\acute{\iota}, \ \tau\acute{\epsilon}\rho\mu\alpha \ \delta'o\mathring{v}\kappa \ \epsilon\mathring{\i}\pi o\iota \ \tau\iota\varsigma \ \~\alpha\nu.$$

If here she says "What different forms of misfortune befall men, and nobody can tell the end of them," she must just have had a new bad experience. Since her last experience before she enters the stage was that her fetters had been dissolved, the nearest event I can think of to which these words might refer is the trouble into which she gets with the first person she meets after she has fled. But, of course, it may belong to a later scene: her sufferings are not yet at an end.

With greater confidence I should like to ascribe two other fragments—fragments 208 and 205—to a monologue of Antiope—two most remarkable sentences that continue Euripides' reflections on the value of knowledge. But I will pass them over now and treat them extensively later.

In the ensuing scenes the mother and the sons must have recognized one another with the help of the old shepherd, but how this was brought about we cannot make out. Though Amphion in the latter part of the play believes that Antiope is

---

[15] Schaal p. 27: "Alterius partis [sc. of the dialogue between Antiope and Amphion], ubi de servitute agitur, fragmenta, cum tam exigua sint et generatim sententiam exhibeant, in ordinem et conexum restituere non possumus."

[16] Hyginus and Propertius testify that the sons before they have recognized their mother refuse to take her up in the house.

his mother, he is not yet convinced that Zeus is his father; only Hermes convinces him of that at the end of the drama.

Approximately in the middle of the play Euripides introduces another chorus—a chorus of maenads that came from Thebes together with Dirke, who had prosecuted Antiope so wildly. It does not seem likely that Dirke comes to this place because she knows that Antiope is here. She would scarcely have chosen maenads as her companions if she wanted to force back Antiope. On the other hand, it seems plausible that maenads by their own free will come to Eleutherai, the renowned sanctuary of Dionysus. And, in fact, a fragment of *Antiope* shows that Euripides has presented a motive precisely why the maenads come just to the poor dwellings of the shepherd: a pillar of Dionysus, wreathed with ivy, is in the rooms of the shepherds.[17] So they may have come simply for some cult action. But perhaps there is more behind it. The speaker of these verses (one might suspect Dirke) perhaps thinks that a shepherd's hut is a place unworthy of such a holy object and may have insinuated that it should be brought to another place. But that is all too uncertain. In any case, as is shown by a fragment of Pacuvius, the maenads came in violent ecstasy,[18] and evil intentions may not have been alien to them, nor to the audacious Dirke.

Somehow Dirke must have found Antiope: she drags her away to tie her to a wild bull.[19] But just in time her sons save

---

[17] The lines are incomplete and perhaps corrupt. The easiest way to restore them seems to be:

ἔνδον δὲ θαλάμοις ⟨ἐν ⌣ οισι⟩ βουκόλων
κομῶντα κισσοῦ στῦλον εὐίου θεοῦ,

—⟨ἐν μικροῖσι⟩?, βουκόλων Wil., *Ar. u. Ath.* 2, 43, 13 (—κόλον mss.)

[18] Pac. fr. 12; Schaal, p. 29, n. 2 thinks that Pac. fr. inc. 4 belongs to the same context. An intended rapture of the sacred stone and its abduction to Thebes had of course to be seen in contrast to the way in which Peisistratos transferred the cult to Athens.

[19] Schaal (p. 50) suggests that fr. 213 might have been spoken by Dirke to Antiope:

κόρος δὲ πάντων· καὶ γὰρ ἐκ καλλιόνων
λέκτροις ἐπ' αἰσχροῖς εἶδον ἐκπεπληγμένους,

her: they bind Dirke herself to the bull and she is dragged to her death. (This is the scene represented in the famous group called the Farnese Bull, in Naples. Euripides had the story told by a messenger.)

The end of the drama (about 130 lines, with some gaps) is preserved on a papyrus found at the end of the last century: Antiope and her two sons reënter the stage. They are informed that King Lykos of Thebes, the brother of Antiope's father, is approaching with his men, and they seek a device to catch Lykos. Amphion says to his mother that it would be definite proof that Zeus is his and Zethos' father if he were to help them now.[20] He admonishes his divine father that he cannot possibly have enjoyed the love of Antiope without feeling obliged to save her and their children now.[21]

Antiope and her sons go into the house, and the chorus announces the arrival of Lykos. Lykos comes in great excitement and asks the chorus where Antiope is and who has helped her to be liberated and to flee into the mountain. He believes, as we hear later, that Dirke is still alive, and he has come to help her.

There follows a gap in the papyrus of more than thirty verses. Where the text is readable again, Lykos and the old

δαιτὸς δὲ πληρωθείς τις ἄσμενος πάλιν
φαύλῃ διαίτῃ προσβαλὼν ἥσθη στόμα.

(cf. Pac. fr. 8 R.³); but perhaps Antiope said this to Dirke. Schaal (p. 50) thinks that fr. 209 may contain words directed to Dirke:

οὐ σωφρονίζειν ἔμαθον, αἰδεῖσθαι δὲ χρή,
γύναι, τὸ λίαν καὶ φυλάσσεσθαι φθόνον.

Indeed it seems very possible that Antiope, remembering her haughty behavior toward Amphion, said something like: "[I now recognize that] I had not learnt to be wise. But one must beware of all excess and stand in awe of the jealousy of the gods."

[20] Rightly Schaal (p. 33) points out that Amphion is not yet utterly convinced of his divine descent. Only Hermes right at the end assures him definitely.

[21] On this kind of "challenging-nouthetetic" prayers cf. A. M. Dale, *Maia* 15, 1963, 31.

shepherd are engaged in a stichomythia. The shepherd per-
suades Lykos that the most important thing to do is to prevent
Antiope from fleeing. Therefore he advises him to place his
soldiers around the house at some distance (and so removes
them from the scene) and assures him that the two sons of
Antiope have died (that is, in the struggle with the followers of
Dirke when Antiope was liberated?). He himself promises to
look after the king's safety if he enters the hut. So Lykos goes
into the house alone in order to kill Antiope with his own hands.

The chorus remains alone on the stage. Soon one hears from
within, the cries of Lykos who is assaulted by Zethos and
Amphion. The door of the house opens,[22] Amphion tells Lykos
that he and his brother have killed Dirke by tying her to the
bull, and that he is going to kill him too.

But suddenly Hermes appears as a *deus ex machina* on the
roof of the house and forbids the brothers to murder Lykos.
He tells Lykos that Zethos and Amphion are in fact the children
of Zeus and that he must take them to Thebes and give them
the supreme power in the Kadmeia. He is also to throw Dirke's
ashes into the fountain of Ares which from then on will bear
the name of Dirke. The brothers shall fortify Thebes and to
the lyre of Amphion the stones and trees will move together
to build the walls. Later they will be held in great honor in the
town. The last words, after Hermes disappears, are spoken by
Lykos: he confesses that he has acted without sound counsel
and that he was in error. He leaves the kingdom of Thebes to
Zethos and Amphion and promises to bury Dirke as Hermes
has ordered. "I dissolve the feuds and all that has been done,"
λύω δὲ νείκη καὶ τὰ πρὶν πεπραγμένα. So the drama finds a
happy end after so many changes of fortune.

It is an action full of tension and surprises, but all this lies
rather outside those passages that have made the tragedy
famous in antiquity.

---

[22] That is, the "ekkyklema rolls out so that the audience may see the twins preparing
to kill [Lykos]. . . . This is the point of ὁρᾷς." T. B. L. Webster (as cited in n. 1
above), l.l. 96.

Now let us consider how the motifs we traced in some former Euripidean tragedies are developed in *Antiope*. Of the two scenes to be examined we shall first take the less important one, which occurs later in the drama, the monologue of Antiope. Later we shall consider the discussion of Zethos and Amphion about the active and contemplative life.

Antiope brings forward a philosophy of her own. In fr. 208 she says, full of resignation: "If I have been neglected by the gods, I myself and my two sons, there is some reason for it [λόγος, sense—something one gives an account of—all this the word implies]. Of all the many mortals some must be unhappy, the others happy."

She feels abandoned by the gods—and specifically by Zeus, who is the father of her sons—but finds a dreary consolation in the insight that human life is like that: some have bad luck (are δυστυχεῖς, have an adverse τύχη), some have good luck.

Antiope has knowledge, but a knowledge quite different from that of Sokrates, which was meant to help man in his problems, to make him "good," to prevent disaster. This knowledge is different too from that gained by "investigation" (ἱστορία) praised by the chorus. It leads only to resignation. Since Antiope is saved after all, this pessimism turns out not to have been justified. But what she says is not merely a blunder. Situations legitimating such thoughts often occur, a fact older poets, too, were aware of.

But Antiope draws new conclusions from such experiences (fr. 205): "I have insight into what I suffer, and this is no small evil. For not to know has a certain pleasure for one who is afflicted by disease; ignorance is an advantage in misfortune." [23]

Antiope again is a "helpless woman," but her ἀμηχανία is not moral weakness. Though words recur here that we have heard from Phaedra, as, for example, φρονεῖν, δυστυχής, κακόν, εἰδέναι, ἡδονή, νόσος, ἀγνωσία (= ἄνοια), their context has

---

[23]   φρονῶ δ' ἃ πάσχω, καὶ τόδ' οὐ σμικρὸν κακόν·
              τὸ μὴ εἰδέναι γὰρ ἡδονὴν ἔχει τινὰ
              νοσοῦντα, κέρδος δ' ἐν κακοῖς ἀγνωσία.

changed completely: both are helpless and ill—but Phaedra's disease was that her insight was too weak to gain victory over her passion; Antiope, in her calamity, does not suffer from such moral frailty, but she does not simply fall back to the ἀμηχανία of Sappho. She feels that she has too much knowledge about her misfortune: insight makes it all the worse. This is not found in earlier characters. For her it would be a certain pleasure (ἡδονή) to know less, for knowledge destroys pleasure, whereas for Phaedra pleasure (*Hipp*. 382 f.) prevents men from acting according to their knowledge.

It seems difficult to explain how Antiope's new ideas about pleasure, illness, and knowledge have developed from those of Phaedra. It becomes easier if we return once more to the objections Socrates raised against the statements of Medea and of the second Phaedra.

Socrates contended: Knowledge about what is really good will overcome pleasure and moral weakness. Man can win true happiness by intellectual efforts. To this Antiope answers, as Phaedra did: Life in reality is quite different. But leaving aside the moral implications and speaking only about happiness she says: It is the natural order of things that some people are to be happy and others unhappy. But once you are unhappy knowledge does not help you—the opposite is true, it makes you all the more unhappy.

Admetus, Medea, and the two Phaedras suffered from moral insufficiency. For Antiope it is not her own deeds which are under question. She has been treated ignominiously by Zeus and by fate. This recalls the situation of Simonides' Danae who, enclosed in a wooden chest with her baby Perseus and driven over the stormy sea complains that Zeus, the father of her son, does not help her. This recalls also the Danae in Aeschylus' *Diktyulkoi*. But these two Danaes do not reflect on the law that some have to suffer and some can rejoice (though Archilochos had said before that human life moves in a "rhythm"), and above all they do not maintain that to be ignorant of one's own situation is a kind of pleasure.

If, as it seems to me, Euripides has developed this new idea in opposition to Socrates' optimistic outlook on the efficiency of knowledge, he is here, of course, in opposition too to the sophists who taught ἀρετή. For you cannot teach *arete* unless you believe that knowledge is good and helpful.

Since the old Euripides uttered a similar skepticism against knowledge in some other passages also,[24] this must have been a matter of special concern to him. But this is left aside for now.

The second and more important scene which has had an immense influence on later thinking is the discussion of Zethos and Amphion at the beginning of the play. To reconstruct this dialogue we have to start from a statement made by the so-called Auctor ad Herennium (2, 27, 43),[25] who says that Pacuvius (and that means his model Euripides too) has in this dispute changed the subject: it began with a controversy on music and shifted to *sapientiae rationem et virtutis utilitatem*.

Indeed the point of departure seems to have been that Amphion sang a cosmogonic hymn[26] starting with the elements —and combining music with philosophy. That is apparently the reason why Euripides did not make the shepherd Amphion sing a conventional pastorale. It may be remembered, too, that at this time the word σοφία comprised poetry as well as philosophy, so that the changing of theme to which the Auctor ad Herennium objects was not as strongly felt at the time of Euripides as in the first century B.C. Zethos reproaches Amphion with the words[27]

κακῶν κατάρχεις τήνδε μοῦσαν εἰσάγων
ἀργὴν φίλοινον χρημάτων ἀτημελῆ,

"It is the beginning of evil if you introduce this Muse that is lazy, wine-loving, and careless about money."

---

[24] *Iph. A.* 924 f., El 294 ff.; cf. *Philol. Suppl.*, 20, 1, 1928, 156 and above, p. 65.

[25] As Schaal (p. 11) rightly emphasizes. Cic. *De inv.* 1, 50, 94, who goes back to the same lecture on rhetorics as the Auctor has abridged the notice so that we don't learn anything new from him. But cf. Dio Chrysost. 73, 10 (Zethos) οὐκ ἀξιῶν φιλοσοφεῖν αὐτὸν (Amphion) οὐδὲ περὶ μουσικὴν διατρίβειν.

[26] Fr. 1023 = 182a N.³

[27] Fr. 184 + ad. 395, see N.³, Suppl. p. 1030.

If Zethos speaks of poetry, he can be thinking only of songs in the symposion where young people waste their time, are given to the pleasure of drinking, and squander their money.

From this point of view, music seems to be related to ἀργία and ἡδονή, laziness and pleasure, that is, to those things that Phaedra made responsible for the fact that knowledge and reason are weak in inner conflicts. But, of course, the differences are great: Phaedra does not make poems, and Amphion who is blamed for laziness and pleasure is, as we shall see, just the man who defends knowledge and intellectual merits: for him there is no inner conflict between ἀεργία and *sophia*, laziness and wisdom. What the others call his laziness is the σχολή he needs for his *sophia*.

Zethos expresses his opinion even more clearly in fr. 187: "A man who has won an honest livelihood but by carelessness gives it up, and because he has pleasure in singing [and dancing] always strives for such things, will be lazy in his house and in the state, and to his friends he will be nothing. For nature is gone, if a man yields [in the inner conflict] to sweet pleasure."[28]

The standards according to which Zethos judges human life are the welfare of οἶκος and πόλις, the house and the state, and the usefulness a man has for his φίλοι. Similar thoughts have been brought forward by others, for example, by Xenophanes. But Xenophanes thought *sophia* was the means to achieve the welfare of the community. For Zethos it has the opposite effect. He maintains that φύσις, unreflecting sound nature, makes man useful. This nature is spoiled, if someone weakly yields to "sweet pleasure."

Amphion must have used the word σοφία or σοφός, as Zethos replies to him (fr. 186):

πῶς γὰρ σοφὸν τοῦτ' ἔστιν, ἥτις εὐφυᾶ
λαβοῦσα τέχνη φῶτ' ἔθηκε χείρονα;

---

28 ἀνὴρ γὰρ ὅστις εὖ βίον κεκτημένος
τὰ μὲν κατ' οἴκους ἀμελίᾳ παρεὶς ἐᾷ,
μολπαῖσι δ'ἡσθεὶς τοῦτ' ἀεὶ θηρεύσεται,
ἀργὸς μὲν οἴκοις καὶ πόλει γενήσεται,
φίλοισι δ' οὐδείς· ἡ φύσις γὰρ οἴχεται,
ὅταν γλυκείας ἡδονῆς ἥσσων τις ᾖ.

"How can something be wisdom, that in reality is a τέχνη [an art, a device] that gets hold of a man with good *physis* [nature] and makes him worse." "Having a good *physis*," εὐφυής, is a word used in animal breeding and means "of a good race, of good stock." These are not new ideas. That the sophists, and among them Socrates, spoil good normal nature, particularly of young people, by their *sophia* was proclaimed about fifteen years before by Aristophanes in the *Clouds* and was a fatal argument against Socrates, less than ten years later. (This argument has been brought forward repeatedly even in our own day against "intellectuals.")

Though Zethos takes over from Socrates the idea that morality gains victory over pleasure and weakness, he radically disagrees with him about what should be the victorious power in man: He does not believe that *sophia* can help in this conflict—for him just the opposite is true: *sophia* spoils man, he is saved by something very irrational. The idea of the εὐφυὴς ἀνήρ and of his *physis* that determines his value belongs to the ideology of the aristocratic society of archaic times. Pindar often mentions the φυά of the right man, but, of course, he does not believe that poetry spoils this "nature" and *sophia* deteriorates man. On the contrary: *sophia* is the highest value he can think of. But he maintains that whoever wants to achieve *sophia* must by birth have the right nature; mere learning can not win real insight.

So Zethos takes up the idea of usefulness from Xenophanes, of *physis* from Pindar, of victory over pleasure and weakness from Socrates. But he eliminates what for all three was a cardinal virtue: *sophia* and knowledge.

Zethos tells us in three verses what his objections to σοφία are, but since this fragment is quoted in Plato's *Gorgias* in a distorted context, I must dwell upon it longer. The text is (fr. 183):

$$ἐν τούτῳ ⟨γέ τοι⟩^{29}$$
$$λαμπρὸς θ' ἕκαστος κἀπὶ τοῦτ' ἐπείγεται$$

---

[29] Suppl. Valckenaer, cf. E. R. Dodds, *Plato, Gorgias*, pp. 273 f.

νέμων τὸ πλεῖστον ἡμέρας τούτῳ μέρος,
ἵν᾽ αὐτὸς αὑτοῦ τυγχάνει βέλτιστος[30] ὤν.

"Each shines in that, and pursues that, and devotes the greatest portion of the day to that in which he most excels" (trans. Jowett).

Kallikles in Plato's *Gorgias* (484 E) quotes these verses after saying: "Whoever makes his appearance in a field alien to him is ridiculous." Hence one should expect the verses to mean: "but he finds recognition and achieves most where he toils"— and this would be an admonition: "the cobbler must stick to his last." But the sense is: "Everybody finds recognition and toils where he is especially good." The original sense of the words becomes clear from Aristotle (*Rhet.* 1, 11, p. 1371b 26) who before quoting the last two verses says: "Since everyone is selfish (φίλαυτος), it follows that all find pleasure in their own things, such as in their deeds and words . . . καὶ ἐπεὶ τὸ ἄρχειν ἥδιστον, καὶ τὸ σοφὸν δοκεῖν εἶναι ἡδύ, since to rule is most sweet, to seem wise is also sweet." It appears that Euripides speaks of the personal pleasure Amphion finds in the pursuit of his individual talents. Zethos does not praise a man who puts all his efforts into a special task. Rather he blames the man who thinks he can indulge in his own self-love and ambition.[31]

Homer already knows that one man is better in one field and another in a different one. The new idea here is that one is conscious of his special faculties and, by his own effort, endeavors to become more perfect.[32]

It has often been maintained that this idea was uttered before by Pindar (P. 2, 72) in his famous γένοι᾽ οἷος ἐσσι μαθών, but I think it was pointed out rightly by Wilamowitz (*Pindaros*, p. 290) that it does not imply much more that what Hector says

---

[30] Sic Plat., *Gorg* 484 E, Aristot., *Rhet.* 1, 11 pp. 1371b; κράτιστος [Plat.], *Alc.* II, p. 146 A, Plut., *De garr.* 22, 514 A, al. It seems to me that fr. 183 has to be put after 187, since 187 would nicely continue 184.

[31] Cf. [Plat.], *l.c.* φιλοτιμούμενον, Plut., *l.c.* φίλαυτος . . . καὶ φιλόδοξος.

[32] ἐπείγεται, cf. fr. 187, 3 θηρεύεται 198, 2 θηράσεται (sic Blass cum pap. Flind. Petr.).

(*Il.* 6, 444) μᾶϑον ἔμμεναι ἐσϑλός: The thought is that a member of a certain society must follow acknowledged standards.[33]

Zethos holds that such individualistic striving for one's own perfection does not serve the community, that such self-assertion (which we found for the first time in Aeschylus' Achilles) is a danger for the state.[34] He concludes his argument by saying (fr. 188): "Follow me, stop your foolishness[35] . . . Do such work as shows that you are reasonable [δόξεις φρονεῖν]: digging, ploughing, watching the herds, and leave to others these dainty artifices [κομψὰ σοφίσματα] that only lead to poverty."

Of course, it is not without reason that Zethos looks upon poetry and all sorts of *sophia* with suspicion. Aristophanes tells us that those who were called *sophoi* in ancient times were in danger of becoming vain impostors and charlatans,[36] and no doubt there were in Athens at that time enough impecunious fellows who wasted their time with κομψὰ σοφίσματα as Zethos calls it. Thus intellectual activity might always seem to be bound up with vanity, whereas sound and unspoiled thinking (φρονεῖν) is to be found among primitive and natural men. Such ideas were later taken up by Rousseau, and through Schlegel and Nietzsche influence the politics even of our day.

Amphion in his answer makes it clear that Zethos did not grasp his meaning and that therefore his arguments are not

[33] Cf. *Philol. Unters.*, 29, 72; W. Burkert, *Gymnasium* 66, 1959, 169. If Pindar had wished to say: "become what you are by an intellectual effort," he would at least have used the present participle μανθάνων and not the aorist μαθών.

[34] Wilamowitz (cf. Schaal, p. 14) rightly attributes fr. 219 to Zethos: "The good man is reticent, the bad man a prattler (ἐκλαλεῖ, cf. 188, 5 κομψὰ ταῦτ' ἀφεὶς σοφίσματα) only for his pleasure (ἡδονή); he is an evil for the community and weakens the state." That corresponds exactly to what Zethos says in other fragments. Again, Aristophanes would not disagree. That arguing is something vulgar Pindar (fr. 180) said long before; for other similar passages cf. Pearson on Soph. fr. 81.

[35] παῦσαι ματάζων, Wil., *Platon* 2, 375 (ματαιάζων in Plat. cod. P et in marg. TW); cf. Dodds, p. 279: "Zethos does not advise his brother to give up music altogether, but to content himself with simple unphilosophical ditties and attend to his livelihood." Perhaps one could think of poems in the kind of Hesiod's Erga. The following πολέμων is corrupt. Schaal writes πραγμάτων with Plato's paraphrase; not very convincing.

[36] Cf. *Greek Poetry and Society*, p. 95.

cogent and his concept of usefulness, pleasure, and wisdom inadequate.

To Zethos' fr. 187 Amphion answers in fr. 198 as follows: "If one has good luck [εὐτυχῶν] and earns a livelihood [βίον κεκτημένος ∼ fr. 187, 1 εὖ βίον κεκτημένος] and by doing so he is not pursuing τὰ καλά in his house (τῶν καλῶν θηράσεται[37] that is, as in a hunt ∼ fr. 187, 3 τοῦτ' ἀεὶ θηρεύεται), then I would not call him blessed (ὄλβιος), but rather a fortunate (εὐδαίμων)[38] guard of money." Amphion has a higher concept of happiness than his brother: it may be useful to look after one's own welfare; whoever succeeds in this may be called "lucky," εὐτυχῶν, and he may even have a fortune in terms of money, but he is not ὄλβιος, fortunate in a higher sense, happy, and blessed. This word ὄλβιος has a religious connotation, like μακάριος or ἰσόθεος "god-like," as we shall see later.

What true happiness is has been discussed since the time of the Seven Sages as we learn from Herodotos' story about Solon and Kroisos. Zethos in many respects stands with Solon and defends the simple life of the peasant or shepherd as against the luxury and refinement of exaggerated cultural achievements. But in the history of Solon and Kroisos true happiness is lasting happiness. Solon shows Kroisos that one cannot determine who is happy until one has seen his whole life; then it may turn out that a simple life has been happy to its very end.

Zethos' argument is different: he measures life according to what a man is trying to achieve. A life worth living is the useful life of an active man who cares about the welfare of his house, his friends, and his state. However, Amphion sets up a different goal: what he calls τὰ καλά, something beautiful and valuable far beyond mere utility, which will make man ὄλβιος, blessed,

---

[37] So Blass rightly with P. Fl. Petr., πειράσεται Stob.

[38] I should not change εὐδαίμονα to εὐήμονα (Buecheler) or εὐδαιμόνων (Bruhn, Schaal, p. 15, 2). εὐδαίμων can have different shades of meaning in different contexts, but the connotation of "rich" is quite obvious and common in prose. Possibly Zethos had used the word in his speech and said that *his* way of life would lead to εὐδαιμονία.

truly happy. We know that he is thinking of poetry and philosophy.

In fact, it is he who takes up the decisive arguments of Solon, but he adapts them to his new situation. In fr. 196 he says:[39] "Such is the life of the miserable mortals: Nobody is in every respect happy [εὐτυχεῖ][40] nor unhappy [δυστυχεῖ]. Why then should we, since we continue our life in an uncertain ὄλβος [fortune], not live in as much pleasure as possible [ὡς ἥδιστα] and without grief." From Solon's insight that life is unsafe, always exposed to be ruined, [41] Amphion draws the conclusion that it is best to seek pleasure where one can find it and to beware of sorrow. He explains this more precisely in fr. 194: "The man who leads a quiet life is a safe friend [ἀσφαλής, not exposed to dangers and ruin] and is the best one for the state. Do not praise dangers.[42] I am not a friend of the daring sailor or the ruler of a state." The quiet life, that is, the *vita non activa*, is not exposed to dangers and therefore not only brings safer and longer happiness, but is the most useful life to friends and to the state. Certainly, Solon would not agree with this argument—he, who took full responsibility for Athens in a dangerous situation—but Amphion soon answers the question of political utility with stronger arguments.

More vital for his case are fragments 193 and 199: "He, who is busy about many things [πράσσει πολλά, is a πολυπράγμων] where it is not his business to be active [μὴ πράσσειν παρόν], is stupid, when he can live inactive [ἀπράγμων] in pleasure [ἡδέως]." "It is a shame that you blame my weak and effeminate body. For if I am able to think rightly [εὖ φρονεῖν] that is better [κρεῖσσον] than a strong arm." Further (fr. 200), Amphion explains more closely why the mind is more valuable than the body. He says: "Insight and cognitions [γνώμαις]

[39] I think there can be no doubt that the fragment belongs to this context (so Nauck, Schaal, p. 16), though the speculations about changing fortune sound similar to what Antiope says fr. 208.

[40] This is an old *topos*, cf. ad Bacchyl. fr. 20 B.

[41] Hdt. 1, 32; cf. 3, 53 τυραννὶς χρῆμα σφαλερόν etc.

[42] So Zethos must have recommended *vivere pericolosamente*.

govern both the state and the house well, and moreover they are a strong help in war. Wise [σοφόν] counsel is victorious over thousands of hands. In the mass of the people[43] ignorance [ἀμαθία] is the greatest evil."

Here Amphion in a surprising way abandons his former view that ἀπραγμοσύνη is the best thing. Now he yields to the argument of utility for house and state, brought forward by Zethos. And the idea that intellectual abilities may be more valuable than bodily strength has been said in Greece ever since Nestor recommended his wisdom or since the quarrel arose about the weapons of Achilles: after his death they were to be given to the second best hero and the Greeks decided to give them to the clever Odysseus and not to the strong Ajax.[44] "One man is worth thousands if he is the best one," is a saying of Heracleitos (fr. 49): εἷς ἐμοὶ μύριοι ἐὰν ἄριστος ᾖ,[45] and there can be no doubt that Heracleitos by ἄριστος means the man who takes part in the λόγος. But nowhere before Amphion's speech do we find this radical and fundamental distinction between body [σῶμα] and intellect [εὖ φρονεῖν].

That the soul is more valuable than the body seems to have been developed in religious circles. I do not want to—and in fact I cannot—go into the details of the intricate question, what hopes the Orphical or Pythagorean sects have cherished for the soul surviving the body, if man had led a pure life.

But Amphion looks down upon the body as inferior, not because his soul is "pure" in a religious sense, but because he has intelligence and knowledge (γνώμη, σοφία, εὖ φρονεῖν). This is philosophy, inaugurated by Parmenides and Hera-

---

[43] Van Groningen, *Mnemos.*, IV, 12, 1959, 134 writes σύνοπλος for σὺν ὄχλῳ, since Gal. 1, 35 K. has σὺν ὅπλοις.

[44] About the further development of the relation between the man of wisdom and the man of deed cf. *Greek Poetry and Society*, p. 40.

[45] This is quoted by Plat. *Gorg.* 490 A though not directly from Herakleitos but by help of tragic verses which Dodds reconstructs to this passage in this form:

κρείσσων γάρ ἐστι πολλάκις τῶν μυρίων
τῶν μὴ φρονούντων εἰς φρονῶν.

It is well possible that they come from the speech of Amphion (fr. ad. 348a N.³).

kleitos, and especially Socratic philosophy as we read it in Plato. This is the basis on which Euripides has built up the distinction between *vita activa* and *vita contemplativa*.

But, alas, we do not get a clear picture of what Amphion means by *vita contemplativa* and what are "the beautiful things" (τὰ καλά), whose pursuit makes a man truly happy (ὄλβιος fr. 198); τὰ καλά sounds more as if it was applied to music than to philosophy, but it may comprise both. At any rate, Amphion must have explained more precisely to his brother, that pleasure (fr. 193, 2) for him is not the enjoyment of a symposion (fr. 184). He praises the freedom of business and the love of a quiet life (ἀπράγμονα fr. 193, 2; ἥσυχος fr. 194, 1) and says he does not want to be a ruler (fr. 194, 4), but this is in clear contradiction to his words that intellect and knowledge are more valuable for government in peace and war than bodily strength.

This difference may have to do with the fact that Amphion, as Horace tells us, yields to Zethos and that in the course of the discussion they come to some agreement. Amphion may have said: my ideal is the pure *vita contemplativa* dedicated to music and philosophy, but you must admit that, if a man wants to be useful to the community, the qualities of the mind are more efficacious than those of the body.

A fragment of Euripides praises the *vita contemplativa* more explicitly than any words preserved from Amphion's speech (fr. 910). It is a choral song and has long ago been assumed to come from *Antiope*:[46]

> ὄλβιος ὅστις τῆς ἱστορίας
> ἔσχε μάθησιν,
> μήτε πολιτῶν ἐπὶ πημοσύνας
> μήτ' εἰς ἀδίκους πράξεις ὁρμῶν,
> ἀλλ' ἀθανάτου καθορῶν φύσεως
> κόσμον ἀγήρω πῇ τε συνέστη

---

[46] Schaal, p. 24. It has often been assumed that Euripides here thinks of Anaxagoras who is said to have praised θεωρία as τέλος of man's life. That is possible. Whether Anaxagoras has discussed the relative values of the different βίοι is less certain.

χῶϑεν χῶπως·
τοῖς δὲ τοιούτοις οὐδέποτ' αἰσχρῶν
ἔργων μελέτημα προσίζει.

"Blessed [ὄλβιος] is he who has been in the school of investigation [ἱστορία] and who does not set out to make the citizens suffer or to do unjust deeds, but rather looks at the unchanging order [κόσμος] of eternal nature [φύσις], in which way it came about and wherefrom and how. With such people never the exercise of shameful deeds will sit down."

In the beginning of Amphion's hymn, where he sings "Aether and Earth, the Mother of all things," we find the "contemplation of the κόσμος φύσεως" that is, the θεωρία, and the question of "how it came together."[47] Even more striking is that here the cosmogonic speculations are linked with the question of what is useful or harmful for the citizens. All this arises naturally from the discussion between Zethos and Amphion, but in a choral song not put into the context of *Antiope* it would be surprising to combine such different things.

If this praise of the philosopher really belongs to *Antiope*, it can scarcely have been put after Amphion's philosophical hymn, because then the chorus would have no reason to enter upon the question of how a man can be useful to his citizens. This question is raised by Zethos and further discussed by Amphion. So it seems to be more appropriate at the end of this scene.[48]

This has an advantage too. Euripides had to conclude the *agon* with a reconciliation of the two brothers, since later they must act in common against Dirke and in favor of their mother Antiope. Moreover, in the following scenes he had only one actor for both, since one of them had to be mute. Euripides chose Amphion as a speaking character so that the audience could follow the actions of the brothers with full sympathy. But then Amphion could not attend the happenings in simple contemplation but had to become active. The praise of the

----
[47] συνέστη, cf. Empedocl. 35, 6 συνιστάμεν' ἄλλοϑεν ἄλλα.
[48] Schaal, pp. 23 f. cautiously puts it here too.

philosopher brought forward once more the importance of the
vita contemplativa, though in the dialogue Amphion had yielded
to Zethos (as Horace puts it),[49] and had conceded that it might
be necessary to take over some responsibility, not merely to remain ἀπράγμων, free from business, altogether.

At the end of the play, Hermes, as a *deus ex machina*, tells
Amphion to take part in the ruling of Thebes, but in a curious
way he shows the superiority of a life dedicated to the muses:
Amphion will build up the walls of Thebes not by corporal
work but by his music. To the sound of his lyre the stones and
trees will move and fit together to form the fortification of the
town. Euripides knew, if any of the Greek dramatists did, that
real life is toilsome and brutal. But here, as in other instances,
he tries to overcome the hardships by taking refuge in a fairy-
tale motif. Perhaps this lyre of Amphion was meant to be a
symbol of the higher power of the muses—but perhaps (who
knows in Euripides?) a bit of irony crept in too.

Zethos says to his brother (fr. 188):[50] "Follow me, stop your
foolishness." So he admonishes him: "You must change your
life, take up the life I am leading." The idea of following a new
track of life appeared for the first time in Aeschylus' *Isthmiastai*,
where the satyrs, serving Dionysus, wished to become athletes
and take part in the games of Poseidon. In the first *Hippolytos*
Phaedra wishes to take part in the hunter's life of Hippolytos
whom she loves, and in the second *Hippolytos* the two different
ways of life were represented by Artemis and Aphrodite.

In *Antiope* each of the two lives is founded on principles
about which one can argue; a discussion becomes possible; each
partner presents his reasons for adhering to his aims. It is a
question of the τέλος, the end of life, for which a man ἐπείγεται
νέμων τὸ πλεῖστον ἡμέρας τούτῳ μέρος, as Zethos puts it (fr.
183), to which end he exerts himself, giving most of the day's

---

[49] Therefore it does not seem very probable to me that fr. 206 belongs to the chorus
as Schaal (p. 18) believes, and with Wilamowitz (Schaal, 18, 3) I should rather give
it to Antiope (see above, p. 74, n. 11).

[50] On this difficult fr., see above, p. 86, n. 35.

time to it. Such a conscious endeavor to put into practice a chosen theory is described by Euripides about the same time in the *Phoenissae*. There, too, two brothers discuss their ways of life, but nothing of this kind is to be found before.

Now it is not the more pleasant life that is at stake (though Zethos insinuates this) as for Aeschylus' satyrs, nor is it passion, as in Phaedra, who wants to give up the old life in order to be united with another person, but here convictions stand against one another—convictions such as in the Achilles of Aeschylus.

In spite of the mythological background, the satyrs of Aeschylus and the Phaedra of Euripides are not determined by religious motives. The satyrs have no special *inclination* for Poseidon, but simply look for a more pleasant life, and Phaedra is far from wishing to be a servant of Artemis when she wants to go hunting with Hippolytos; she is merely following her passion. So in both instances a personal desire determines the form of life.

Though the *vita activa* and *contemplativa* are secular forms of a *bios*, there is still a strong religious motive effective here. This becomes especially apparent in the μακαρισμός of the chorus. *Makarismos* is a ritual form of praise for a man who has achieved something superhuman and has therefore gained god-likeness. We shall have to investigate this more thoroughly in the next chapters. For the moment it is sufficient to say that a *makarismos* of the kind we find in *Antiope* apparently has its origin in some religious sects. In early poetry we find a different form of *makarismos*, that is, a man may be praised because he takes part in the sphere of the gods on account of a special situation (such as a wedding) or a single achievement (such as a victory in the games).

I would like to return to the obscure field of early Greek mystery cults, on which I touched for a moment when I spoke of Amphion's assertion that the soul was more valuable than the body. The *makarismos* of the chorus somehow reflects old *makarismoi* of those initiated into some mysteries.

I mention here the two oldest examples. One, which goes back to about 700 B.C., is found in the Homeric hymn to Demeter, the other is a fragment of Pindar.[51] At the end of the hymn we read (480 ff.):

ὄλβιος ὃς τάδ' ὄπωπεν ἐπιχθονίων ἀνθρώπων·
ὃς δ' ἀτελὴς ἱερῶν, ὅς τ' ἄμμορος, οὔ ποθ' ὁμοίων
αἶσαν ἔχει φθίμενός περ ὑπὸ ζόφῳ εὐρώεντι

"Happy is he among men upon earth who has seen these mysteries; but he who is uninitiated and who has no part in them, never has lot of like good things once he is dead, down in the darkness and gloom" (trans. Evelyn-White).

Pindar's words are (fr. 137):

ὄλβιος ὅστις ἰδὼν κεῖν' εἶσ' ὑπὸ
χθόν'· οἶδε μὲν βίου τελευτάν, οἶδεν δὲ διόσ-
δοτον ἀρχάν.

"Blessed is he who has seen these things before he goes beneath the hollow earth; for he understands the end of mortal life and the beginning given of god" (trans. J. Sandys).

The first point common to these two *makarismoi* and to the hymn in the Antiope is that the blessed one is praised not in one single situation but for a new life that he has begun through knowledge. But in the mysteries the blessed one has "seen" something; that returns again and again in the *makarismoi* of the mysteria, and it may be recalled that the highest form of initiation in Eleusis was called ἐποπτεία. Once somebody has experienced this "vision" (whatever it may be that he saw in the rite of initiation), he belonged to the group of the blessed. The chorus of Antiope, however, says that he is blessed who got ἱστορίης μάθησιν, that is, who has been in the school of investigation. This word, which the Ionians used for their research in geography, ethnology, and "history," implies inquiry by interrogating a witness. It is not revelation but investigation, not a passive attitude, but a mental activity such

---

[51] Other examples have repeatedly been put together, cf. Nilsson, *Gesch. d. gr. Religion*, I², pp. 666 ff., who gives a full interpretation of the Pindar fragment pp. 674 ff.

as men became conscious of only in the fifth century B.C. It is a similar inner endeavor as we found in the speech of Zethos, when he said (fr. 183, see above p. 84) that man toils to be as perfect as possible, devoting most of his time to this task.

The second point of comparison is that the "blessed" are expected to lead a pure life. But a pure life in the mystery religions is more a negative than a positive qualification. Originally it did not mean striving for good deeds, but rather abstaining from pollution, and thereby winning ὄλβος, which originally meant wealth,[52] so that the pure life made man happy in the sense of εὐτυχής or εὐδαίμων as Amphion uses the words. Certainly there is a marked change in what was considered to be "purity." The magic belief, for example, that a defilement could be cured by some ritual washing was replaced by moral notions, and a decisive step taken by the mystery sects was that they made a distinction between body and soul. I quote only the saying σῶμα σῆμα, which means that the body is the grave of the soul. The conclusion drawn from this was that one had to look after the happiness of the soul more than after the happiness of the body, and that happiness of the soul was more lasting than that of the body.

We find similar ideas in the speech of Amphion. He holds φρόνησις (thinking) in higher esteem than corporal strength (fr. 185), he praises a happiness that is higher than material wealth (fr. 196), he aims at something beautiful, τὰ καλά (fr. 198), and at some wisdom, τὸ σοφόν, as we may infer from his brother's answer (fr. 186). But this surpassed even the moralistic ideas of Orphic or Pythagorean sects.

Let us look at the high ethical standards of the song of the initiated in Aristophanes' *Frogs* 457 ff.:

μόνοις γὰρ ἡμῖν ἥλιος
καὶ φέγγος ἱλαρόν ἐστιν,
ὅσοι μεμυήμεθ᾽ εὐ-
σεβῆ τε διήγομεν
τρόπον περὶ τοὺς ξένους
καὶ τοὺς ἰδιώτας

---

[52] Nilsson, *op. cit.*, pp. 666 ff.

"For us alone the Sun and the Light is cheerful, for us who are initiated and have led a pious life towards private people [i.e., those who do not hold a public office] and proxenoi [i.e., who are not full citizens]."[53]

It is especially remarkable that not only full citizens are admitted to these mysteria. This is an important step toward the humanitarian view that all men have equal rights. But, nevertheless, the moral ideas pronounced here are essentially those developed by Solon; they can be formulated only negatively: being just means: not to be unjust, not to commit crimes or to do anything that might pollute the soul. And here, as in Zethos' speech, the usefulness for the citizens is the criterion of the proper life as it had been taught long before by Xenophanes.

Euripides mentions such Orphic ideas as early as in *Hippolytos*. When Theseus is convinced that his son has tried to rape Phaedra, he calls him a follower of Orpheus who pretends to be chaste, without a taint of evil (σώφρων καὶ κακῶν ἀκήρατος: 949), but in reality only boasts with his "lifeless food"[54] and uses solemn words for plotting sin.

The scepticism of Theseus toward the Orphics does not question the value of a "pure life," but questions the genuineness of the convictions: Hippolytos pretends to lead a pure life, but in reality does not; he is an ἀλαζών and charlatan. This moral problem is similar to that raised in *Alcestis:* there to live for one another in the family was recognized as good, but the question was whether one really lived up to this ideal. In *Antiope* it is no longer taken for granted that the blessed life really is a better life; for Zethos it is not a life under divine guidance, but corruption: κακῶν κατάρχεις τήνδε μοῦσαν εἰσάγων, "it is the beginning of evil, when you introduce this Muse."

Though the chorus sees the blessed life of contemplation against the background of the mystery sects, its value cannot

---

[53] Cf. 327 ὁσίους ἐς θιασώτας, 357 ff. against βωμολόχα ἔπη, στάσις, κέρδη ἴδια, δωροδοκία, πρόδοσις etc.; all those who take part in such things the chorus bids ἐξίσθασθαι μύσταισι χοροῖς.

[54] Curiously enough, he attributes the vegetarian life of Orpheus to the hunter Hippolytos.

be shown by the simple assertion that purity is better than defilement. It has become doubtful which is the best life.

This takes us back to the wish to change one's life. The satyrs of Aeschylus and Phaedra wished a "better" life according to their circumstances, but that was not the "best" life, in a principal and absolute sense. Certainly Hippolytos leads a "purer" life than Phaedra, but Aphrodite makes it clear that his is not a perfect life. Zethos thinks his life the best life, and so he tries to persuade Amphion (fr. 188): ἀλλ' ἐμοὶ πιθοῦ, παῦσαι ματᾴζων, "follow me, stop your own foolishness." This kind of *propaganda fidei* we could expect from an adherent of a religious sect.[55]

Amphion undoubtedly claimed the opposite. So the question of the best life which was decided for the initiated by the simple statement: "Open your eyes and you will recognize what the pure life, the best life is," becomes a matter of discussion, of secular arguments, of philosophical decision.

The dialogue between Zethos and Amphion is not really connected with the action of the play. Of course we may be deceived by the fact that only a small part of the tragedy is preserved, but I do not see how the different opinions about active and contemplative life could have had an effect upon Zethos' or Amphion's attitude toward their mother—particularly since Zethos is a mute person in the later development of the drama.

This is different from what we saw in the older plays. Even in the contemporary *Phoenissae* the dispute between Eteocles and Polyneices about might and right is much more closely linked with the plot. For Eteocles not only *speaks* as a defender of might, but he acts accordingly, and the same is true for Polyneices who in theory and practice stands on the side of right.

This shows that Euripides in his old age becomes more interested in philosophical questions. Yet he does not proclaim a one-sided philosophical dogma, but expresses the thesis as

---

[55] A. D. Nock, *Conversion*, 1933, 26 ff.

well as the antithesis. We cannot identify his personal convictions with those of Zethos or Amphion any more than with those of Hippolytos or Phaedra. He shares the pleasure in the δισσοὶ λόγοι with some of the sophists, and he, as a dramatist and poet, sees opinions as characteristic of living persons. But it cannot be denied that *Antiope* fell into two very different parts, one rather sophisticated, the other an exciting action of primitive *coups de théâtre*, appealing to an unsophisticated audience.

Euripides was influenced by the philosophy of his time; he was deeply worried by its problems, but found no solace in the solutions suggested. On the other hand, he caused the philosophers to take up these questions. Plato, Aristotle, Dikaiarchos, and many others saw in the choice between the *vita activa* and the *vita contemplativa* the fundamental decision about man's task.

In later times the *vita contemplativa* of a philosopher was considered a blessed life, and his pupils bestowed superhuman honors on the founder of a philosophical school as, for example, on Plato or Epicurus. But people pursuing an active life have been much more successful in being recognized as god-like. Just at the time when Euripides wrote his *Antiope* the Greeks began to look upon successful politicians or generals as blessed and divine persons.

V

A Unique Satyr Drama, Python's *Agen:* Structure and Dating

In the following chapters I should like to discuss a strange play that is almost unknown and which—and this strikes me as even stranger—is considered by the few students who do know it to be by no means unique, indeed, not even worthy of note. Only eighteen lines of this drama have been preserved together with one or two short remarks in the work of the author who quotes these lines. These remarks are not consistent, and the curious result has been that scholars have held those remarks which are right to be wrong and those which are wrong to be right—that, in any case, is what I hope to demonstrate. As a result, one has appreciated neither the exciting artistic quality nor the political significance of this play which can be extensively reconstructed from the few lines we have.

The subject of our discussion is the satyr drama *Agen* by Python, an otherwise apparently unknown poet.[1] Already in antiquity it was doubted whether Python was really the author; the play was even ascribed to Alexander the Great—scarcely with any justification, as will be shown, although it is true that it was written by someone in Alexander's nearest entourage.

---

[1] Athenaios calls him Καταναῖος ἤ Βυζάντιος. Steffen (see p. 101 n.) calls attention to the orator Python of Byzantium who was in Philip's service and took part in Alexander's campaigns (but see Berve, *Alexanderreich*, II, No. 677).

Athenaios (596 A), the only author to write about *Agen*, speaks of it as a small satyric drama[2] and says it was performed at a Feast of Dionysos on the Hydaspes (Jhelum), that is, in 326 B.C. during Alexander's campaign in India, roughly at the easternmost point which the Greeks ever reached in antiquity. A fabulous distance! A famous historian has disputed the idea that Alexander can have had a satyr drama performed in his camp, a play which would have had to have been specially written for the purpose, and the philologists as far as I can see have almost all believed him. But we must decide for ourselves after we have taken a closer look at the lines which have been preserved. Here they are:[3]

> ἔστιν δ' ὅπου μὲν ὁ κάλαμος πέφυχ' ὅδε
> †φέτωμ' ἄορνον, οὐξ ἀριστερᾶς δ' ὅδε
> πόρνης ὁ κλεινὸς ναός, ὃν δὴ Παλλίδης
> τεύξας κατέγνω διὰ τὸ πρᾶγμ' αὐτοῦ φυγήν.
> 5   ἐνταῦθα δὴ τῶν βαρβάρων τινὲς μάγοι
> ὁρῶντες αὐτὸν παγκάκως διακείμενον
> ἔπεισαν ὡς ἄξουσι τὴν ψυχὴν ἄνω
> τὴν Πυθιονίκης . . .

> 8a   . . . ἐκμαθεῖν δέ σου ποθῶ
> μακρὰν ἀποικῶν κεῖθεν, Ἀτθίδα χθόνα
> 10   τίνες τύχαι †καλοῦσιν ἢ πράττουσι τί.
> B. ὅτε μὲν ἔφασκον δοῦλον ἐκτῆσθαι βίον,
> ἱκανὸν ἐδείπνουν· νῦν δὲ τὸν χέδροπα μόνον
> καὶ τὸν μάραθον ἔσθουσι, πυροὺς δ' οὐ μάλα.
> A. καὶ μὴν ἀκούω μυριάδας τὸν Ἅρπαλον
> 15   αὐτοῖσι τῶν Ἀγῆνος οὐκ ἐλάσσονας
> σίτου διαπέμψαι καὶ πολίτην γεγονέναι.
> B. Γλυκέρας ὁ σῖτος οὗτος ἦν, ἔσται δ' ἴσως
> αὐτοῖσιν ὀλέθρου κοὐχ ἑταίρας ἀρραβών.

1 sq. πέφυκεν ὁ δ' ἐφέτωμα: init. Dindorf || 3 λαὸς: Casaub. || 5 δή νυν? || 7 ἀξιοῦσι: Casaub. || 10 κραίνουσιν Steffen

[2] σατυρικὸν δραμάτιον. This word is used by Plut., *Dem.* 4, 320e, for the Βάταλος of Antiphanes (fr. 57, C A F. 2, 35).

[3] For the Greek text, see below, p. 105 ff. The most important literature on *Agen* is: Beloch, "Die Aufführung des Agen," *Griechische Geschichte*, IV: 2, 434 ff. Suess-v.

Here where the reeds are growing is an entrance to the underworld, and here to the left the famous harlot's temple which Pallides had built and has chosen as a place of exile in atonement for his past affair [with her]. When some of the Persian μάγοι [*magi*] saw him lying there in distress, they persuaded him that they could conjure up the soul of Pythionike.

Later there follows this dialogue:

A: I should gladly hear from you, as I live far away from there, what conditions are like in the Attic country and how the people fare.

B: When they maintained they had won a life as slaves, they had enough to eat. Now they have only their pea mash and fennel to eat, but no wheat bread at all.

A: And yet I hear that Harpalos sent them over thousands of bushels of corn, no less than Agen once did, and that he has been made an honorary citizen.

B: This corn is a payment on account for Glykera. Perhaps it will be the earnest for their own destruction and not for the hetaira.

Before going into the subject matter, I should like briefly to discuss the metrical form, because the way in which a Greek poet treats his meters is always an important yardstick for measuring his skill and education. So, first, let us ascertain from these iambic trimeters whether this unknown poet has anything artistic and significant to offer.

A good satyr drama should on the whole keep to the iambics as they are used in tragedy. It has been maintained that the iambics of *Agen* are more like the looser form found in the comedy and that such a mixture of style, taken from two genres, was no great recommendation for the play. In fact, there are some deviations which at first suggest this. Above all, there are instances of the resolution of *ancipitia* or *brevia* in the iambs which, though taboo not only in tragedy but also in the satyric drama, are common in comedy. But if we look more closely, the whole business takes on a different light: the resolution of

Blumenthal, *Hermes*, 74, 1939, 210–221. Hommel, *ibid.*, 75, 1940, 237. W. Steffen, *Aus der altertumswissenschaftlichen Arbeit Volkspolens*, 1955, 36–43. Steffen is also responsible for the latest edition: *Satyrographorum Graecorum Fragmenta*, Poznań 1952, 251 f. G. Schiassi, *Dioniso* 21, 1958, 83–94.

the first *anceps* in the proper name (17: Γλυκέρας) would not cause offense in any tragedy. In addition, the discipline of the verse might also excuse the double short syllable in the first *breve* in the proper name Πυθιονίκης (8). In the other instances where double short syllables occur in the *anceps* (6: διακείμενον) or in the *breve* (16: διαπέμψαι, variant: παραπέμψαι;[4] 14: μυριάδας), the double shorts consist of ι plus a short vowel (each time after a long syllable) as in Πυθιονίκης. These four instances would disappear, however, if we were to accept the prosodic anomaly that an ι before a vowel after a long syllable was pronounced as a consonant (= y). There has been much argument whether such prosodic license was permissible in Greek tragedy.[5] But however much one may otherwise hesitate to accept them, we cannot ignore them here, for it is too striking that the instances (apart from the proper noun Glykera) are so equally placed. This can scarcely be chance,[6]

---

[4] διαπέμψαι is without doubt the correct reading as is generally acknowledged. διαπέμπειν "send over" frequently in the papyri (for evidence see Preisigke).

[5] Cf. Christ, *Metrik* § 39, Maas § 120, Schwyzer *Gr. Gr.*, I, 244 f.; Dodds on Eur., *Bacch.* 998 ὄργια says: "apart from the word καρδία (κάρζα?) thrice in Aesch. I know no certain instance of this synizesis in tragedy." I must admit I cannot defend ὄργια as metrical licence. I agree that dochmii such as ⌣ ⌣ — — ⌣ — cannot be doubted, but the examples quoted by Dodds, unlike Bacch. 998, do not respond to ⌣ — — ⌣ —. Barrett on Eur., *Hipp.* 761. Blumenthal (p. 218) draws attention to Eur., *Cycl.* 154. Cf. Soph., *Ai.* 258, *El.* 142, *O.C.* 1466, 1479.

[6] Cf. Dorian Ζάλευκος, Macedonian (?) Σέλευκος. Deviations from this scansion are line 4 διά = ⌣ ⌣ and line 11 βίον = ⌣ —||, both as usually found in tragedy. The end of line 6 παγκάκως διακείμενον is reminiscent of comedy (e.g., Aristoph., *Pl.* 80 ἀθλίως διακείμενον, Men., *Per.* 248 τῷ κακῶς διακειμένῳ, fr. 130 ῥυπαρῶς διακειμένῳ (otherwise fr. 642). In tragedy the verb only occurs once in the form διάκειμαι (Eur., *Tr.* 113). Python has therefore taken over the participle at the end of the line from comedy because he could adapt it to his prosodic principle. By using the essentially tragic adverb παγκάκως he has given it a stylistic lift. Line 11 ἔφασκον δοῦλον ἐκτῆσθαι βίον is reminiscent of Soph., *Trach.* 301 f., where Deianeira says to the chorus of captive Trachiniae:

αἱ πρὶν μὲν ἦσαν ἐξ ἐλευθέρων ἴσως
ἀνδρῶν, τὰ νῦν δὲ δοῦλον ἴσχουσιν βίον.

This is apparently the only place where δοῦλον βίον is attested; as the two words are found at the same place in the line together with the contrast between past freedom and present slavery, we may be justified in taking it as a quotation. For quotations from Sophocles see below pp. 105 and 106. Cf. also [Eur.] *Rhes.* 701 κέκτηται βίον.

and it is likely that here Python was following his own pronunciation or that of his age or district rather than classical models.

The violation of Porson's law in lines 3, 16, and 18 could also be a sign of the metrical treatment usually found in comedy; as comedy breaks the law once nearly every five lines, this would correspond more or less to the frequency here. But this kind of thing, although not nearly so frequent, is not exactly rare in the satyr drama. Finally, line 5 has no caesura; caesuraless lines normally have a diaeresis in the middle of the line (in Aeschylus and Sophocles approximately twenty-five instances; Euripides more frequent—about one hundred, but always with elision [cf. Maas, *Metrik*, § 100]; but it is not found here). For that reason I should be inclined to write δή νυν for δὴ τῶν.

Versification and prosody betray therefore a poet who on the whole keeps to the classical satyr drama, but does not shrink from breaking new ground in details. As a result we shall neither be expecting something of exquisite quality nor something entirely worthless. The author is also, as will be shown, a tolerably cultured man who quotes Sophocles at least twice in eighteen lines.

This "happy medium" is particularly propitious for an attempt at reconstruction, because neither the bad nor the really excellent passages can be reproduced. The bad ones cannot be reproduced because one cannot be sure that what we have really means what it says; the excellent passages because they are beyond guessing. And so I shall venture here a bit further than I did with Aeschylus and Euripides, and hope I will not be producing a rabbit out of a hat.

In order to reach a firm foundation we must test all assertions for their maximum carrying power. Athenaios mentions *Agen* twice: in 13, 586 he quotes lines 14–18, where Harpalos, the principal figure in this play, is mentioned by his right name, and a little later he says (596 A) that Python also called Harpalos "Pallides." He quotes first lines 1–8a, and then lines 8b–18. The question whether something is missing between these two quotations or whether they followed directly one another must be left to later. Harpalos was a close friend of Alexander's, the offspring of a princely family and one of the most powerful administrators in Alexander's kingdom, for Alexander had put him in charge of the financial administration of Persia. In this play Harpalos is attacked for helping two *hetairai* to fame and fortune, thereby causing a considerable scandal. These two women were Pythionike, for whom he built a temple after her death where she was to be worshiped as Aphrodite Pythionike,[7] and Glykera, to whom he had royal honors done and on whom he spent vast sums of money.[8] Python, therefore, gives Harpalos, punning on his name, the nickname Pallides, which means son of Phallus.[9] The title of the play was *Agen*, and we are no doubt correct in deriving this name as *nomen agentis* from ἄγω.[10] Here it is certainly Alexander who is meant,[11] because in line 15 we read that Harpalos had given the Athenians no less grain than Agen— and it was in this way that Alexander had won over the Athenians at the beginning of his reign. If the play was called *Agen*,

---

[7] This cult name is handed down by Theopompus (*F Gr Hist.* 115 F 253).

[8] For evidence see below p. 124 f.

[9] A. Meineke explains this correctly (*Analecta critica ad Athenaei deiphosophistas*, Leipzig, 1867, 280 f.). Admittedly he wanted to write Φαλλίδης, but then the relation to the name Har-palos would be lost. (Cf. Suess, p. 216 and Steffen, p. 38.) According to Macedonian pronunciation one would have to expect Βαλλίδης (Schwyzer, *Gr. Gr.*, 1, 69 ff.), just as an ἄσωτος is called Βαλλίων in Axionikos fr. 1, 2 (2, 412 Kock). Cf. also βαλλίον Herond. 6, 69 and the Ballio of Pseudolus, but "since the κοινή π and φ, τ and ϑ, κ and χ are often confused in Egypt and Asia Minor" (Schwyzer, 1, 204). At all events Cicero is able to find the name Sardanapallus insulting (*Rep.* 3, p. 104, Ziegl). Names like Φαλλίδης, Φαλλίων, Φαλλῖνος, Πόσϑων, Σάϑων, Κερκίδας really occurred frequently (Bechtel, *Hist. Pers.-Namen* p. 482). Schiassi, *op. cit.* see n. 3, above, pp. 89 f. quotes Aristophanes' *Triphales* (fr. 542–557), possibly a nickname for Alcibiades. L. Robert, *Noms indigènes*, 1963, 18 ff.

[10] For word formation, cf. Blumenthal, p. 216; Schwyzer, *Gr. Gr.*, 1, 487. Proper names of this type are Χαιρήν, Μνασήν (these in Bechtel, *Hist. Pers.-Namen*), Ἀρχήν Hdn., 1, 14 Lentz(where Lobeck conjectures ἀχήν), πυϑήν e.g., Thuc. 7, 1, 1, etc. For ἄγειν = to be a military leader, cf. P. Chantraine, *Études sur le vocabulaire grec*, Paris, 1956, 90 f. Now cf. J. and L. Robert, *Bull. épigr.* 1963, no. 234.

[11] Blumenthal, p. 216.

Alexander must have appeared in it personally. But that we shall leave till later.

It strikes us at once that the lines that have been preserved come from the beginning of the play, but they cannot be the first words of the prologue, as has been thought. The δέ at the beginning speaks against this, for in Greek plays people do not enter while conversing.[12] The beginning of Sophocles' *Electra,* which Python quotes and parodies (3), makes this abundantly clear. In Sophocles' play, Orestes, who has been taken abroad as a small child after his father's murder, enters with his old tutor who has brought him back to Mycenae. The tutor, after addressing him (and thereby introducing him to the audience), shows him his old homeland: "here to the left is the famous temple to Hera," οὐξ ἀριστερᾶς δ' ὅδε Ἥρας ὁ κλεινὸς ναός (7 f.). Python makes out of this: "Here to the left is the famous harlot's temple," οὐξ ἀριστερᾶς δ' ὅδε πόρνης ὁ κλεινὸς ναός.[13] Beforehand, the speaker, according to the analogy of the tutor's words, must have said: We are in Babylon (for there, according to Theopompus' evidence [115 F 253] stood the temple to Pythionike). He will also have introduced himself and his partner in some way.

On the left of the stage the famous harlot's temple; on the right, however,—and this comes earlier in the text—is something designated as ἄορνον. Unfortunately the previous word is corrupt,[14] but its meaning is clear, for this is likewise a quotation from Sophocles. The word ἄορνος occurs only once before Python, and a thoroughgoing grammarian, the Atticist Pausanias,[15] has evidently only found it once in Attic writing—

---

[12] A beginning with ἀλλά as in Aristoph., *Lys.* or Menander's *Eunuch* is something else. For the whole question cf. Ed. Fraenkel, *Beob. zu Aristophanes*, pp. 103 f.

[13] λαός ms., according to Sophocles with certainty corrected by Casaubonus.

[14] πέφυκεν ὅδ' ἐφέτωμα, init. corr. Dindorf. Apparently written as prose, as Steffen has seen (he believes it to have happened *before* Athenaios. I did not have the opportunity to check the ms.).

[15] α 127 (Erbse): Ἄορνος λίμνη περὶ Τυρσηνίαν. (Ἀρτεμίδωρος? suppl. Erbse) δέ φησι καὶ ἐν Κύμῃ τῇ Χαλκιδικῇ Ἄορνον λίμνην εἶναι, περὶ ἣν πεφυκότων πολλῶν δένδρων μηδὲν τῶν ἀποπιπτόντων φύλλων ἐμπίπτειν εἰς αὐτήν. εἶναι δὲ νεκυομαντεῖον ἐν ταύτῃ τῇ λίμνῃ Σοφοκλῆς ἱστορεῖ. Maximus Tyr. 8, 2 tells of a λίμνη Ἄορνος in Greater Greece with a μαντεῖον

in Sophocles. What he has to say on the meaning of the word
fits in so perfectly with the singular situation we have before
us here that the dependence on Sophocles cannot be disputed,
especially as the other Sophocles quotation follows directly.[16]

Pausanias says that Sophocles (fr. 748 P. = 682 N.²) had
mentioned the Ἄορνος λίμνη, the *lacus avernus* in Italy, saying
that on its banks there was a *necyomanteion*, a place where one
could conjure up the dead. Sophocles had transferred the
Nekyia of Odysseus there.[17] Python's play also deals with a
conjuring up of the dead,[18] for we read a few lines later that
some barbarian *magi*, when they discovered Harpalos so downcast in the temple of his *hetaira*, persuaded him to allow them
to bring up for him the soul of Pythionike from Hades.

We have therefore a set of clear stage directions: left, the
temple in which the unhappy Harpalos is dwelling; right, the
entrance to the Underworld; this is, we are told, surrounded by
reeds, and as theatergoers we realize that behind the reeds the
soul of a dead person is hidden who will appear some time. We
soon learn that it will be the spirit of Pythionike. Needless to
say, Pythionike will then speak with her lover who will come
out of the temple for this purpose.

Before this, the barbarian sorcerers will enter—μάγοι in the
plural, not just one sorcerer. The only people who appear on
the Greek stage in numbers are the chorus—in the satyr

ἄντρον where ψυχαγωγοί conjure up the dead and places the Nekyia of Odysseus here.
Cf. Strab. 244. All this seems to be dependent on Sophocles (cf. Pearson on this). Some
have thought that here Ἄορνον, the stronghold on the Indus, is meant (Diod. 17, 85),
over which Harpalos had been satrap (cf. e.g., C. B. Gulick in his Loeb translation of
Athenaios ad loc.), but how could that be on the stage "where this reed grows"? I
should not even see an allusion to this place in our passage.

[16] On the possibility of a further Sophocles quotation see above p. 102, n. 6.

[17] E. D. Phillips, *Journ. Hell. St.*, 73, 1953, 56. The saga of Orpheus and Eurydice
was located at another λίμνη ἄορνος in Thesprotia (Paus. 9, 30, 6).

[18] The substantive belonging to ἄορνον cannot be reconstructed. φέτωμα, which is
left if we take off ὅδε, produces nothing. στεφάνωμα (Steffen) is active, not passive;
moreover the double short syllable in the anceps is doubtful (see above p. 102). The
best is still Meineke's ἕλωμ(α) after *Od.* 14, 474 ἂν δόνακας καὶ ἕλος. Compare πύλωμα
with πύλη, πύργωμα with πύργος (but there we have πυργόω), ῥίζωμα with ῥίζα (ῥιζόω),
ῥάκωμα with ῥάκος (ῥάκωμα recorded before ῥάκος), ἕλκωμα with ἕλκος (ἑλκόω), etc.

drama, therefore, the Satyrs. Here they played, accordingly, Oriental priests and sorcerers.[19] What we infer in this way from the suggestions in our text becomes a certainty because it produces an action that is typical of the satyr drama. Since early times such scenes had occurred in nearly every possible variation—scenes in which the Satyrs caused some person, chiefly female, to appear suddenly out of the ground. Ernst Buschor has identified such scenes on vases.[20] For example, the Satyrs in Aeschylus' *Diktyulkoi* make Danae come out of the wooden chest in which she has come across the sea or in Sophocles' *Ichneutae* the mountain nymph Kyllene out of her cave.

By relating Sophocles' Aornos scene to the *magi,* Python, of course, puts the conjuration of the dead in a dubious light. But at the same time he produces a scene which we may

---

[19] The Magoi, in Herodotus a Median tribe, were for the Greeks mostly magicians, tricksters, and seducers.

[20] "Feldmäuse," *Sb. Bayr. Ak.*, 1937, 1. His starting point is Aesch. *Sisyphos Drapetes* (fr. 380 M). The chorus asks, ἀλλ' ἀρουραῖος τίς ἐστι σμῖνθος ὧδ' ὑπερφυής; then Sisyphos appears—moreover like Pythionike here or Dareios in the *Persae*—from the Underworld. The conjuring up of the dead in Aesch., *Psychagogoi* (p. 87 N² = fr. 475 M) probably used (like the Sophocles play mentioned) Odysseus' Nekyia; J. van Leeuwen, whom Nauck (trag. dict. index p. x) agrees with, would like to call this too a satyr drama, but that remains uncertain. The anapaests of the papyrus in Oslo (*Symbol. Oslo*, 31, 1955, 1 ff.) which are accompanied by musical notation give an account of a conjuring of the dead; line 8 reads: ἀνέβη δ' ἐπὶ φέγγος Ἀχιλλεύς. Irmgard Fischer, *Typische Motive im Satyrspiel*, doctoral dissertation, Göttingen, 1958, 53 ff. quotes the corresponding scenes but has nothing new to say about them.

A conjuration of the dead at a λίμνη recurs in Aristophanes, *Av.* 1553. On Eur. fr. 912, a conjuration of the psychai in anapaests, spoken, of course, by the chorus, Wilamowitz (*Kl. Schr.*, 1, 191) writes, "origin unknown," but in his private copy occurs the note in his own hand, "satyr drama"; one might be reminded of Euripides' *Sisyphos*, the satyr drama of the Trojan tetralogy of 415 B.C., but the theme is a conventional one and the plural, psychai, speaks against it, not to mention the fact that here apparently Sisyphos emerges from the Underworld under his own steam. Cf. also H. D. Broadhead, *The Persae of Aeschylus*, 1960, 302–309. A. Gercke, *Rh. Mus.*, 47, 1892, 319, has tried to gain a similar scene of a satyr drama out of Diog. Laert. 6, 9, 1: according to Hippobotos, Menedemus came up from Hades as an Erinys. Gercke thinks this was a scene from the satyr play *Menedemos* by Lykophron. But in fact it is a blunder for Menippus, cf. Croenert, *Kol. u. Men.*, 1; Wilamowitz, *Hermes* 34, 1899, 631 (*Kl. Schr.*, 4, 102, 1); K. v. Fritz, *RE.*, see under "Menedemos," 794, 64.

imagine as colorful, burlesque, and good theater. Just as the
Persians in Aeschylus' play conjure up the spirit of Dareios
with strange calls and rhythmic uproar, the necromantic sorcerers, in Oriental costume, probably staged here an exotic
ceremonial, and if Kyllene in the *Ichneutai* complains of the
disturbance, we may be sure that the Satyrs did not behave
any more decorously. The result was certainly amusing and
lively.

The *magi* were the obvious role for the chorus of Satyrs,
not merely because they performed necromancy—this, by the
way, seems to be one of the oldest instances, if not the oldest,
where they appear as conjurors of the dead[21]—I mention the
magus Mithrobarzanes in Lucian's *Menippus*—but they were
also grave watchers like those whom Alexander came across at
the tomb of Cyrus in Pasargadae.[22] Moreover, this was a
splendid chance for the Satyrs to deck themselves out. All in
all, then, a happy invention which, in many respects, kept to
the traditions of the satyr drama but nevertheless modified the
old themes in a startling fashion.[23] In lines 4–6 (which have
caused interpreters some trouble and at which I shall take a
look in more detail later) so much is certain: the sorcerers
intend to call up Pythionike to oblige Harpalos. Therefore he
must still be on the spot.

It is not certain whether the second group of lines quoted
by Athenaios follows the first without a break. Athenaios introduces the second group of lines as follows: "in the following
passage (ἐν τοῖς ἑξῆς) the poet calls Harpalos by his right
name." This does not necessarily mean that it follows without
a gap. Nauck prints the lines as though nothing were missing.

---

[21] Cf. Hopfner, *"Griech.-aeg. Offenbarungszauber"* I (*Stud. z. Palaeogr. und Pap.-
Kunde,* ed. Wessely, XXI, 1921), Indices under "Nekromantie."

[22] Arrian 6, 29, 7 and 11: Aristob. *F Gr Hist.* 139 F 51.

[23] For this reason Steffen's opinion (p. 43) in accordance with his conception of
Lykophron's *Menedemos* and Sositheos' *Daphnis* seems to me rather unnecessary: He
assumes "that *Agen* did not contain any real action either, but only portrayed the
events in which Harpalos was concerned in the form of a prolonged dialogue between
Python and the other . . . speaker."

In fact, the last words of the first passage and the first words of the second produce together a faultless trimeter, but the caesura after the second *anceps* which separates the two passages is so usual that we can draw no definite conclusion. The contents, however, support the idea that there is a short gap.[24] I should nevertheless like to keep to Nauck's numbering of the lines.

This second passage evidently continues the exposition of the satyr drama. While somebody was relating what had happened in Babylon, now somebody (and there seems to be nothing against the assumption that it is the speaker of the first lines) asks what things are like in Athens. The poet skillfully brings the answer of the interlocutor, who has obviously just arrived in Babylon from Athens, around to Harpalos' second *hetaira*, Glykera. An important part must have been allotted to her later in the play, otherwise she would scarcely have been mentioned in such a way in the exposition; and if Harpalos is characterized from the start by his nickname as a rake, we must expect him to continue his dissolute life with Glykera.

Evidently Glykera is already on her way to Babylon from Athens, because the conversation is obviously steering toward this. First, however, we are given important information about the political and economic situation in Athens, all of which gives us some idea of the play's polemic purpose.

The resident of Babylon asks: "I live far away from there.[25] What are things like in Athens?"[26] The newcomer answers: "As long as the Athenians maintained they were living the life of slaves, they had enough to eat. Now they only have pea mash

---

[24] Thus Suess (p. 211) in agreement with Koerte, *N Jbb.*, 1924, 217 ff.

[25] Cf. Herondas 1, 13 μακρὴν ἀποικέω at the same point in the line. Therefore a quotation perhaps: Gyllis apologizes for being such a rare visitor.

[26] Ἀτθίδα χθόνα τίνες τύχαι καλοῦσιν ἤ πράττουσι τί; which is what the mss. have. κραίνουσι (Steffen p. 29, n. 3) is preferable to κρατοῦσι (Kaibel); it is also palaeographically a little better, especially as in the prototype N with short third hasta evidently occurred (cf. 1. 3 ΛΑΟΣ for ΝΑΟΣ). The change of subject τί πράττουσι (sc. οἱ Ἀθηναῖοι or more generally as in λέγουσι, or something like it) is acceptable: the tragic diction is therewith made to fit in with the colloquial tone.

and fennel." The Babylonian answers: "I hear that Harpalos sent them thousands of bushels of corn, no less than Alexander [in the past] and that he has been made [as a result] an honorary citizen [of the city]."[27]

The Athenians could maintain that they were leading the lives of slaves after having had to submit to Alexander. Their dependent existence, but also with it the good life, came to an end (that is what Python means, to be sure) when Alexander was in the East.[28] Then Harpalos had stepped in and supplied the Athenians with more grain than Alexander had done. Python insinuates, therefore, that Harpalos is supporting the Athenians at the moment of their desertion from Alexander. This he finds all the more outrageous as Harpalos is really only intent on procuring a beautiful *hetaira* from Athens.

Athenaios says before he quotes these lines that Python mentioned Glykera as already living with Harpalos (ὡς οὔσης παρ' αὐτῷ). This, however, contradicts the text as we have it, and is the result either of careless reading or refers to a later scene in the play. The Babylonian (as we might as well call the first speaker) has indeed heard of Harpalos' generous gift of corn to the Athenians. He knows that he had been made an honorary citizen, but judging from the Athenian's reply, the deal has not yet been finally settled. He says: "This grain was for Glykera—it is probably a guarantee payment for their misfortune and not only for the *hetaira.*"[29] ἀρραβών is the deposit which lapses when a purchase does not materialize. The Athenians sell Glykera, so to speak, in part payment and expect as πορνοβοσκοί, brothel keepers, after the "deposit" further supplies of grain,[30] as soon as the wares are well and truly in the hands of the buyer. But, the speaker says, we shall see that

---

[27] πολίτης: "honorary citizen," cf., e.g., Busolt, *Griech. Staatskunde,* 2, 1926, 945.

[28] It is not clear what he is referring to here, for until 326 B.C. Lykurgus appears to have kept the Athenian finances in good repair. There is also no suggestion as far as I can see of a famine or the like in Athens. It is possible that Python was more interested in dramatic and polemic effects than in the facts.

[29] I agree with Steffen (p. 40) who places a comma and not a colon in line 17.

[30] As Blumenthal rightly says, p. 220.

they have not received money for the *hetaira* but for their misfortune. (The fact that the agreement has a hitch in it— they are *selling* the hetaira but *buying* the misfortune—we shall simply have to accept.)

Python has obviously brought in the "deposit" so that the deal may appear as not yet complete but nevertheless awaiting an early settlement. Harpalos, it is true, has done all there is to do to procure a new mistress, but he is still lying disconsolate in the temple of Pythionike. Python needs such a situation for the conjuration. But Glykera must make her entrance soon, and this presupposes that the deal is well on the way toward completion. We shall also see that Python will take the opportunity of giving the Athenians a piece of his mind and thus expressing his own political convictions. As one calls up the dead, especially at a λίμνη ἄορνος, in order to learn something about the future, it is probable that Pythionike made prophecies, thereby preparing the audience further for Glykera's entrance.[31]

Let us now return to the question of whether the second group of lines quoted by Athenaios (8b–18) followed directly on the first (1–8a). This is improbable, because several things must have been said somewhere not only about the setting of the play but also about the man who has just come from Athens. The jump from the temple and the sorcerers to the question on the state of affairs in Athens also appears far too abrupt.

But if Athenaios introduces the second group with the words ἐν τοῖς ἑξῆς, we cannot separate it too far from the first, and it is very probable indeed that the character who describes the setting of the action in the first lines is the same who asks the questions about Athens in the second.

From what we have said, the structure of the play would look something like this: At the beginning two persons appear (the parody of the line from Sophocles' *Electra* infers a com-

---

[31] Suess (p. 213) has also observed that the conjuration of Pythionike prepares the way for the appearance of Glykera.

parable situation, and lines 1–8a would not fit nearly so well into a monologue). One of them knows all about Babylon. Blumenthal (p. 217) considers it could be Silenus,[32] but he would scarcely speak of the Satyrs (and I am sure that it is they who are concerned) as "some barbarian *magi*," especially as he himself, as we expect, plays the part of a kind of chief sorcerer. Blumenthal also discusses the possibility of that person being a tourist guide. It seems to be probable that he is a servant of Harpalos, at all events a Greek, because he calls the sorcerers barbarians; but we cannot be sure.

The other speaker who comes from Athens is certainly no Athenian—would he otherwise say such scornful things about his fellow citizens? (and, in addition, refer to them in the third person?)—but, as Blumenthal rightly says, a Greek with Macedonian sympathies. Nearer than that we cannot get either.

After this initial dialogue the chorus of Satyrs will have entered with anapaests and staged the conjuration of Pythionike. Harpalos must have entered after them in order to hear about the impending arrival of Glykera. Next she appeared, and since we know that Harpalos wished that Glykera be treated like a queen, we may be sure that he caused the satyrs to show due reverence to the *hetaira* by προσκύνησις and all the other acts of adoration. No doubt that made brilliant theater. Finally, as Blumenthal has concluded (p. 218) from the title, Agen-Alexander[33] enters and sends the Satyrs packing together with Harpalos and his Glykera. This gives us a typical ending for a satyr drama.

But in order to understand the meaning of this ending we must first clear up an important preliminary question. When did Python put the play on? Athenaios gives two contradictory

---

[32] Admittedly he is thinking of a Silen monologue as in the *Cyclops.*

[33] Perhaps Agen-Alexander-Dionysus, as T. B. L. Webster suggests to me. In 324 B.C., Demades proposed in Athens that Alexander, as second Dionysus, should be accepted among the gods of the state (cf. Berve, *Alexanderreich*, II, No. 132) and probably at the same time Protogenes painted him as Dionysus together with Pan (*ibid.*, II, 329).

assertions: either it was performed on the Hydaspes, that is to say in India, more or less at the easternmost point that Alexander reached, or after Harpalos "had [already] fled to the sea and deserted," that is, after Alexander had returned and when Harpalos must have been afraid of being punished for his mismanagement of things. In my opinion the first date, 326 B.C., is the right one, and the second, 324 B.C., the wrong one, although almost everyone who has recently expressed an opinion assumes the contrary.[34] As such an assumption seriously detracts from the appreciation of the political significance of the play, not to speak of its quality, I shall go into the matter in greater detail.

The modern dating of *Agen* was fixed by Julius Beloch who inserted a section into his *Griechische Geschichte* (IV: 2, 434 ff.) on the performance of *Agen*. In his opinion it is obvious "that Alexander in the summer or autumn of 326 B.C., when he stood on the banks of the Hydaspes, had better things to do than organize theatrical performances for which, moreover, he had none of the minimum properties required; and in any case there is no mention made of such a celebration in our accounts of Alexander's campaign."

The scholar sitting at his desk may well in all seriousness suppose that Alexander had not the time during his campaign to organize the performance of a satyr drama and, what is more, a small δραμάτιον, as Athenaios calls it.

Alexander was, however, anxious to raise the morale of his troops with athletic contests and feastings. We also know that he received reinforcements in men and arms on the Hydaspes (from Harpalos incidentally—Curt. 9, 3, 21), and the organization of the new men and material must have taken up enough time and might well have aroused in the men feelings similar to those experienced by soldiers in our day: "Nobody knows how bored we are, bored we are, bored we are, and nobody seems

---

[34] The only exception of which I am aware is Schiassi, *op. cit.* (see n. 3, above), p. 83, but he does not draw the necessary conclusions.

to care, oh!" And so from a military point of view there was every reason for staging a Dionysiac feast.[35]

The argument that he had no theatrical properties available would be relevant if he were putting on a Wagner opera but not a Greek play. In any case, we are told what is needed for a performance of this dramation: on the one side a few reed bushes, behind which an actor can be hidden, on the other the wall of a temple with a few pillars and a door. It would not be very difficult to get hold of that.

Beloch believes further that when Athenaios says of Python and his play, ὅπερ ἐδίδαξεν Διονυσίων ὄντων, this presupposed that a full-scale Dionysos feast was necessary for the performance. There are only two questions we can ask there: Why? Why not?

The following argument of Beloch's is the most significant: line 4 mentions Harpalos' φυγή, but Harpalos did not take to flight until after Alexander's return. As we have already mentioned, Athenaios draws the same conclusion from this line. But if line 4 mentions a φυγή that Harpalos undertook, it cannot be referring to his famous flight after Alexander's return (autumn 325 B.C.: Diod. 17, 108, 6). The sentence has been variously interpreted.[36] Of Harpalos we read: after the construction of the temple, κατέγνω διὰ τὸ πρᾶγμ' αὐτοῦ φυγήν. I read this in the same way as Suess does: "he condemned himself to exile as a result of his deed"; that is the usual way of construing καταγνῶναι, with the accusative of the punishment and the genitive of the person. By "deed" Suess (and Olivieri) understands the building of the temple in Babylon. But Harpalos did not run away because he had built a temple. That was, at the most, an instance of his extravagance. The decisive point was that Alexander returned and called him to

---

[35] W. W. Tarn, *Alexander the Great*, 1, 126, says of Alexander: "He discovered the value of amusements in this respect (i.e., in preserving the troops' morale) and held athletic and musical contests at every important halting-place." Arrian, *Ind.* 18, 12 expressly mentions that Nearch's fleet was assembled on the Hydaspes and that before sailing ἀγῶνές τε αὐτῷ (the river god) μουσικοὶ καὶ γυμνικοὶ ἐποιοῦντο.

[36] See especially Suess, p. 212, and Steffen, p. 39.

account. But it seems to me to be clear enough to what kind of exile Harpalos condemned himself. Some sorcerers have seen him in his desolate condition in the temple. Therefore he did not run away to the sea, as Athenaios says, but banished himself to the temple of Pythionike,[37] evidently in order to escape the pleasures of this world. That an exile can find refuge in a temple we have known since Alkaios' days. There he is to meet the spirit of Pythionike. The *lacus Avernus* on the stage would be pointless if his deceased girl friend were not to appear there. The supposed purpose, however, of the conjuration is to console Harpalos in his misery, although it is, of course, the announcement of Glykera's coming that does this. The whole action of the play becomes meaningless if Harpalos has already made off for Greece. It is naturally easy to understand how the φυγή mentioned here was later identified with Harpalos' much more famous flight—but Python could naturally not foresee such a misunderstanding.

τὸ πρᾶγμα, the reason why Harpalos banished himself into the temple, is therefore the whole love story, the "affair."[38] Evidently Python was intent on stating the exposition in broad outline first of all, leaving the details till later. As we do not know the details, we have to rely somewhat on guesswork. But again and again we are shown that we may confidently take what Python says at face value.

Finally Beloch tries to make Athenaios' assertion that *Agen* was performed on the Hydaspes agree with his view that it is not the river in India that is meant but another Hydaspes in Media, the river of which Vergil writes (*Georg.* 4, 211):

Praeterea regem non sic Aegyptos et ingens
Lydia nec populi Parthorum aut Medus Hydaspes
Observant.

---

[37] Steffen rightly understands the φυγή into the temple, but without ridding himself of the opinion that *Agen* was performed after Alexander's return.

[38] There are frequent examples of a similar use of πράττειν, πρᾶξις, πρᾶγμα, since Pind. fr. 127: μὴ πρεσβυτέραν ἀριθμοῦ δίωκε, θυμέ, πρᾶξιν. E.g., Aischin. 1, 132 of Harmodios and Aristogeiton τὸ πρᾶγμα ὡς συνήνεγκε τῇ πόλει, Men., *Epitr.* 344 f. ἐὰν δ' οἰκεῖον ᾖ αὐτῷ τὸ πρᾶγμα and B. A. van Groningen, *Pindare au Banquet*, pp. 126 f.

Vergil is here extolling the bees: even Orientals, he says, do not honor their kings as bees do. Was there really, as Servius says,[39] a Hydaspes in Media, or has Vergil made a mistake in placing the Indian river so far westward? A Hydaspes in Media is not mentioned anywhere else—except by Petronius (123, 239), *Pompeius repertor Hydaspis,* but the general opinion rightly says that he had this from Vergil.[40] It seems to me frankly nonsensical to assume that Vergil should have named a completely unknown river here where he is speaking of the great Oriental kingdoms and their rulers, especially as poets otherwise speak of the Hydaspes as a "characteristic" river. But, then, it is always the Jhelum in Upper Punjab which owes its fame to Alexander:

> Horace *c.* 1, 22, 8: the Syrteis, the Caucasus
> > *vel quae loca fabulosus* [!]
> > *lambit Hydaspes.*[41]
>> Lucan 3, 236: *Vastis Indus aquis mixtum non sentit Hydaspen*
>> 8, 227: *qua rapidus Ganges et qua Nysacus Hydaspes accedunt pelago*

In both cases the subject is the Far East, and Agathias AP. 4, 80 (*ca.* A.D. 500) calls the river so as well. It would therefore appear obvious, as most students now agree, that Vergil was simply guilty of a blunder—it merely does not seem to have penetrated to the few who have worked on Python's *Agen.*

But even if the Hydaspes in Media which Vergil mentions did exist, it is absurd to assume that in a story concerned with Alexander the Great a Hydaspes which is not expressly called Median Hydaspes is not the famous river in India.

There can be no doubt that Athenaios' assertion about the Hydaspes, which is generally rejected, is in fact correct; whereas

---

[39] *Medus Hydaspes, fluvius Mediae.*

[40] The *Schol. Vat.* has *potest videri poeta Hydaspen Medum dixisse iure belli* etc. The cautius formulation here shows that the author had no concrete facts to go on.

[41] For context, cf. E. Fraenkel, *Horace,* p. 185.

conversely the note on Harpalos' flight, which is accepted, is in fact false. This means that *Agen* was not performed somewhere in Persia in 324 B.C. but in the Punjab in 326 B.C.—and further, the political situation was quite other than is generally held to be the basis of the satyr drama. In order to clarify this we must consider Alexander's situation, Harpalos' position, and the mood of the army. By a happy chance we are, I believe, able to suggest where Python obtained his information, what this information was, and to judge what he made of it.

VI

Python's *Agen:*
Sources, Political Slant

IF IT IS TRUE that the satyr drama *Agen* was
performed in Alexander the Great's military camp in India in
326 B.C. and not, as is generally believed, two years later somewhere in Persia after Alexander's return, the political slant of
the play, the polemics, and the mockery of Harpalos take on a
different aspect. Harpalos fled in disgrace from a magnificent
job as soon as Alexander returned. After that date such a
lampoon against Harpalos would have been rather like letting
off a damp squib. Two years earlier, on the other hand, an
attack on the most powerful man that Alexander had left
behind in Persia, was a highly significant, not to say a dangerous, undertaking. But the play was not only concerned with
a personal altercation but, as we shall see, with a fundamental
problem of the new kingdom that Alexander had created.

If we assemble the details which our earlier analysis yielded
and supplement them with a few extra dates, we can summarize
the action of *Agen* as follows: Harpalos' *hetaira* Pythionike is
dead. He, therefore, erects a temple to her in Babylon where
she is worshiped as Pythionike Aphrodite. This temple stands
on one side of the stage; on the other is an entrance to the
Underworld grown around with reeds. During the exposition,
two persons appear, one who is a resident of Babylon and knows

all about what has been going on there, the other a man from Athens. The first character relates that Harpalos is lying in the temple inconsolate at the death of his mistress and that Persian *magi* had offered to conjure up the soul of Pythionike from the Underworld for him. The other man reports from Athens that Harpalos had paid a deposit of a great quantity of grain on the price for a new *hetaira*, Glykera, and as a result had been made an honorary citizen. From then on the action of the play must have been approximately as follows: the Satyrs appear dressed as Persian *magi* and call up the soul of Pythionike at the entrance to the Underworld. Harpalos, who was on hand in the temple, must then have spoken with Pythionike, who will have consoled him with the news that his new *hetaira* was on her way. In order to make the theme of the second mistress dramatically effective—and there is no doubt it was—she must have made an appearance and, considering what we have already learned of Python's artistic capabilities, we can trust him to have turned to good account the motifs which the figure of Glykera offered (that she was expecting *proskynesis*, for instance) converting the whole into lively scenes with the Satyrs and with Harpalos.

As the title of the play is *Agen*, and as it is most likely Agen is Alexander, he probably appeared in person at the Python must, therefore, have anticipated his triumphant to Babylon, and Alexander will have brought the Sa reason and Harpalos to account—a final scene typical satyr drama. These partly airy speculations are meant that what we do know of the subject matter is consiste typical satyr-drama themes.

We owe our knowledge of the political content of more or less to chance. We possess part of a repo informed Alexander the Great of Harpalos' doings king and his army were in the East. This report is th from Chios" written by the historian Theopompus which have been handed down to us by Athenaios man to whom we owe what little knowledge we hav

And the parts we have are precisely those which deal with Harpalos' relationship with Pythionike and Glykera.[1]

Whether Python had direct access to Theopompus' account and whether it perhaps was his only source, we cannot say. But the points in which they agree and disagree are so significant that it is worth making a comparison.

In fact Athenaios (13, 586 C) quotes "The Account of the Letter from Chios" for his information about Glykera and the "Letter to Alexander" (13, 595 A) for his information about Pythionike. Apparently no one seems to doubt that he is referring to the same publication. The double title leads us to believe that Theopompus wrote a report to Alexander from Chios on the situation in the West and later published the letter in an article which portrayed the circumstances in which the letter was written as a justification or the like.

The letter has been called an "agent's report,"[2] but Cicero's

---

[1] It is impossible for us to divine either how Athenaios came by the quotations from Theopompus or whether he found them together or separate. When Athenaios says after a Theopompus quotation: τὰ ὅμοια δ'εἴρηκε καὶ Κλείταρχος ἐν ταῖς περὶ 'Αλεξάνδρου 'Ιστορίαις (13, 586 C = F Gr Hist. 115 F 254a), our first thought is naturally whether this Theopompus quotation (and then the other two in Athenaios) was not obtained through Kleitarchus and whether he perhaps did not use the "poetaster" who took part in the Indian campaign as part of Alexander's retinue. (This is W. W. Tarn's view: *Alexander the Great*, Cambridge, 1948 [2 vols.], e.g., 2, 55.) There were, however, enough intellectuals with Alexander in the East, one of whom, if it were not Python himself, could have brought *Agen*, or at least part of it, back to the West with him. We can accept Theopompus' account of Harpalos in his letter from Chios as trustworthy, because we hear of his expenditure on Pythionike from other sources. Dikaiarchus (fr. 21 W. = Athen. XIII 594 E) gives an account of Pythionike's μνῆμα on the sacred road. This was seen by Pausanias as well (1, 37, 5) and Plut., *Phokion* also mentions it. (It must have been a cenotaph, as the real tomb was in Babylon.) Poseidonios' fragment (87 F 14 = Athen. XIII 594 E) is not clear. According to him Harpalos had robbed Alexander of large sums of money, fled to Athens, and spent so much out of love for his hetaira Pythionike, ἐκφέρων τε αὐτὴν ἐπὶ τὰς ταφὰς . . . τεχνιτῶν τῶν ἐπισημοτάτων χορῷ μεγάλῳ καὶ παντοίοις ὀργάνοις καὶ συμφωνίαις παρέπεμπε τὸ σῆμα. This must refer to Babylon and was probably confused by Athenaios. Cf. also Philemon's Βαβυλώνιος fr. 16 (2, 482 Kck):

βασίλισσ' ἔσει Βαβυλῶνος, ἂν οὕτω τύχῃ.
τὴν Πυθιονίκην οἶσθα καὶ τὸν ''Αρπαλον.

[2] W. Otto in Berve, *Alexanderreich*, II, No. 365. On the other hand, Laqueur (*RE.*, see under "Theopompus," 2219, 25 ff.) is correct; for Theopompus does not exactly

term Συμβουλευτικόν is more apposite,[3] a political pamphlet in which the conceited quinquagenarian historian gave his king advice. The extant passages read as follows (Ath. 13, 595 A = F Gr Hist. 115 F 253, trans. by C. B. Gulick): Theopompus, when denouncing in his *Letter to Alexander* the licentiousness of Harpalos, says:

Consider and learn clearly from our agents in Babylon how he ordered the funeral of Pythionike when she died. She, to be sure, was a slave of the flute girl Bacchis, who in turn was a slave of the Thracian woman Sinope, who had transferred her practice of harlotry from Aegina to Athens; hence Pythionike was not only triply a slave, but also triply a harlot. Now, with the sum of more than two hundred talents he erected two monuments to her; the thing that surprised everyone is this, that whereas for the men who died in Cilicia defending your kingdom and the liberty of Greece neither he nor anyone else among the officials has as yet erected a proper tomb, for the courtesan Pythionike the monument at Athens and the other in Babylon have already stood completed a long time. Here was a woman who, as everybody knew, had been shared by all who desired her at the same price for all, and yet for this woman he who says he is your friend dared set up a shrine and a sacred enclosure and has called the temple and the altar by the name of Aphrodite Pythionike, by one and the same act showing his contempt for the vengeance of the gods and endeavoring to heap insult on the offices you bestow.

And further (Ath. 13, 586 C = F 254 a):

Of Glykera Theopompos says, in his treatise *On the Chian Letter*, that after the death of Pythionike Harpalos summoned Glykera from Athens; on her arrival she took up her residence in the palace at Tarsos and had obeisance done to her by the populace, being hailed as queen; further, all persons were forbidden to honour Harpalos with a crown unless they also gave a crown to Glykera. In Rossos they even went so far as to set up an image of her in bronze beside his own ⟨and Alexander's⟩.

---

pull his punches as far as Alexander is concerned (see below, p. 124). The fact that he later published the letter does not, however, prove that it was not originally an agent's report.

[3] *Ad Att.*, 12, 40, 2 (= 115 F 251).

And finally (Ath. 13, 595 D = F 254 b):

After the death of Pythionike, Harpalos sent for Glykera, who was also a courtesan, to come to him, as Theopompos records, adding that Harpalos forbade anyone to offer him a crown unless he crowned this harlot also. Further he has set up a bronze portrait of Glykera in Rossos, Syria, where he purposes to rear a monument to you and to himself. More, he has given her the privilege of residing in the royal palace at Tarsus, and permits her to be worshipped by the people and hailed as queen and honoured by other emoluments which were more fittingly bestowed upon your mother and your consort.

These sentences torn from their context give no help in dating Theopompus' letter from Chios.[4] He evidently presupposes the same situation as *Agen*. Pythionike has been dead for some considerable time; the μνήματα both in Athens and Babylon have been completed for some time (F 253: πολὺν ἤδη χρόνον ἐπιτετελεσμένον). In *Agen*, it is true, Pythionike cannot have been dead that long, because Harpalos is still downcast at her death. But this, naturally, does not mean that Theopompus' report must have been written later because, for dramatic reasons, Python had to advance Pythionike's death as closely as possible to what he had to say about Glykera. Nor can we assume that Theopompus' letter was written later, because he writes about Glykera's life in the palace at Tarsos, whereas the play presupposes her to have been first in Athens and then goes on to portray, at the most, her arrival. From what Theopompus has to say, it becomes even clearer than it already was that mention of Glykera at the beginning of the play is meant to prepare her entrance later and that Glykera can only be given the necessary dramatic weight beside the dead Pythionike if she appears even more impressively as a *courtisane arrivée*— all of which could be more easily achieved by doing her royal honors, as Theopompus says was the case.

---

[4] Laqueur (*RE.*, see under "Theopompus," 2220, 21) dates it, without sufficient reason, *ca.* 324 B.C. In our attempt at dating what Theopompus says, we must take into account the time it took for news about Harpalos to reach him in Chios and the even longer time it took his letter to reach India.

We have already established 326 B.C. as the date of performance. If we then keep to 324 B.C. as the date for Theopompus'
letter, the moral-political indignation at Harpalos' dissolution
and extravagance would come two years *post festum*. Theopompus could undoubtedly have imparted further outrageous
details; but two years later Theopompus would not send any
news by portraying a Harpalos again, when Python had already
made fun of him two years before on the Hydaspes. It is much
more plausible that the letter was written earlier.

The details of Python's account tally also closely with
Theopompus' letter. In the one Pythionike is referred to as
πόρνη, in the other as τρίπορνος; in the one her ναός is mentioned, in the other ἱερὸν καὶ τέμενος and ναός and βωμὸς
Πυθιονίκης Ἀφροδίτης. But this proves little; it is perhaps significant that both quote figures to support their accounts of
Harpalos' extravagance: according to Theopompus (F 253), he
spent two hundred talents on Pythionike's memorial, whereas
Python says he sent the Athenians thousands of bushels of
grain (more than Alexander) as an advance payment for
Glykera. Theopompus describes Harpalos' and his friends'
marks of honor, Python probably did likewise: in the few
extant lines he mentions the temple to Pythionike and Harpalos'
honorary citizenship of Athens, and so he probably also mentioned the honors done to Glykera.

But apart from all this, if Theopompus describes certain
things to Alexander who is in the Far East and Python knows
about them, it is no great step to the conclusion that he came
by the information in Theopompus' letter. It seems idle to
indulge in speculation as to how Python procured the information and what role he may have played at Alexander's court;
there are several possibilities. Theopompus and Python not
only agree in condemning Harpalos' behavior toward his
courtesans, they also exploit the political capital of his affair
in much the same way. And yet their political colorings are
clearly distinct.

Theopompus writes to Alexander (115 F 253): "Of those who

have fallen for your kingdom and the freedom of the Greeks," none has yet received a memorial. Python, on the other hand, speaks of the freedom of the Athenians with unconcealed derision: when they maintained they were slaves, they had enough to eat. Now they must go hungry. Theopompus believes therefore (and demands it) that the Macedonian dominion could be reconciled with the freedom of the Greeks. Python evidently considers a stricter dominion over the Greeks by the Macedonian king appropriate. Theopompus represents the traditional-ideological opinion of the Greeks inasmuch as they were prepared to make the best of the Macedonians; Python is evidently more in sympathy with the practical Macedonian point of view.

But both are to the same degree concerned with more than Harpalos, his ambition, and his bad taste; Harpalos represents for them both a burning political question, indeed a fundamental problem of Alexander's kingdom. This is much more clearly so with Theopompus than with Python, but there is so much less of the latter's text extant. All that Theopompus relates about the *hetairai* has but one aim: to show that Harpalos is claiming for himself and for them honors to which they are not entitled—but each time he adds to whom such honors would be due.

After stating what vast sums Harpalos has squandered on the memorials to Pythionike, he adds: "Everyone is amazed [he quotes, therefore, public opinion] that up till now neither Harpalos nor any other of the senior officials has decorated the tombs of those who have fallen for your kingdom and for the freedom of the Greeks in Cilicia" (i.e., at Issus, seven years before), and, further: "He who purports to be your friend has ventured to erect a shrine to Pythionike Aphrodite; thus he disregards the vengeance of the gods and tries to drag your name through the mud" (115 F 253). Of Glykera he says (F 254 b): "At Rossos in Syria he erected a bronze statue to Glykera, in the same place where he is planning to put up a statue to you and himself. He has also allowed her to live in the palace of Tarsos and has the people prostrate themselves before her, address her as queen, and honor her with other gifts that are the due of your mother and your wife."

It is less easy to discern how Python dealt with such things in his play. He makes fun of Pythionike's temple and Harpalos' honorary citizenship, of Glykera's honors too, we may be sure. Besides, as her entrance could not be allowed to contrast—to her disadvantage—too greatly with the appearance of the spirit of Pythionike Aphrodite, which the audience had seen shortly before, the most obvious thing for the sorcerer-satyrs to do was to honor Glykera like a Persian queen by prostrating themselves before her. The chorus of Persian necromancers could be just the thing for such a purpose, and it probably led to further similar scenes.

Theopompus, however, is not only concerned with the honor due. When he hints that the soldiers who had fallen in the war would have been worthier of Pythionike's honors, but had not received them, when he expresses the opinion that Alexander's name was being dragged through the mud when a temple was dedicated to Pythionike Aphrodite, and says that Glykera was receiving honors which (in part, at least) were due to Alexander's mother Olympias or the queen Roxane, there is something more behind his remarks—something which, as we know, was a subject of heated and frequent discussion precisely at the time of Alexander's campaign and a central problem of Alexander's new kingdom: the ruler cult. Theopompus is far more interested in Alexander and his kingdom than in Harpalos, his ambition, and his bad taste. And the fact that Python calls his play *Agen* implies this.

In order to understand what Python's attitude to this was, we should have to know above all how he treated the royal honors shown to Glykera, and especially the *proskynesis.* That part of the play is irreparably lost. But that Python *did* set about this problem I should like to assume, because—apart from the reasons already given—the *proskynesis* granted her by Harpalos is the one really topical, interesting, and important thing about her. And it is inconceivable that Python, who had laid such stress on divine reverence in Pythionike's case, should have ignored the most exciting and shocking thing about Glykera.

The political significance that these courtesans thereby assume can be estimated by surveying how far such honors usually went at the time, what was more or less the accepted practice, and what was out of the question. We must also consider whether we can discern different groups of opinion on the matter and, finally, discover how much Alexander himself may have enjoyed being confronted with such things by Theopompus and what he may have thought of seeing them before his own eyes in Python's play. I can only stress here the few things which are important for our play, features which reveal its relation to the conception of the ruler cult, and, especially, those which bring out what was singular and novel in Harpalos' behavior.

Pythionike is honored as dead, Glykera as alive. Although these two forms of veneration are beginning to flow into one another at the time, they must first be considered separately. When Theopompus, in his letter to Alexander, contrasts the shrines to Pythionike with those to the soldiers who fell at Issus, he is thinking that the dead can receive the honors of a hero, in the same way as Simonides (fr. 5 D) had said of the fallen at Thermopylae:

$$\text{εὐκλεὴς μὲν ἀ τύχα, καλὸς δ' ὁ πότμος,}$$
$$\text{βωμὸς δ' ὁ τάφος, πρὸ γοῶν δὲ μνᾶστις,}$$
$$\text{ὁ δ' οἶκτος ἔπαινος.}$$

"Glorious is their fortune and noble their lot; for grave they have an altar, for laments remembrance, and for pity praise." Such gratitude for services rendered to the fellow citizens could be bestowed also upon an individual person as the founder of a city, the deliverer in time of need, and others. He could be worshiped as a hero after his death, and the worship of such a hero could be the principal manifestation of the political unity of a particular community; especially for smaller groups, the *phylai*, families, hero worship was a unifying bond.

Groups could feel their solidarity, because they were established by a hero, or even because their members looked upon the hero as an ancestor. Thus the Homerides honored Homer, the Asklepiads Asklepios, the potters Keramos, the judges Lykos.

The cult which Harpalos created for Pythionike differs in fundamental points from the actual hero worship. A ἱερόν, a τέμενος, a βωμός, a sanctuary and an altar are all part of the cult of the dead, but the sacrifice is centered on the tomb. Here, on the other hand, the dead woman has become an Olympian goddess, Pythionike Aphrodite, and so she has a proper temple (ναός).

The deification of a hero had also occurred in earlier times; a mythical hero especially could be honored as a god, as, for example, Apollo Hyakinthos and similar instances show.[5] But the earliest evidence of contemporaries honoring someone under a human-divine double name appears to be the mention of altars to "Zeus Philippios" in Eresos around 334 B.C.[6] But here not only is the designation different, for "Zeus appertaining to Philippos" is less offensive than the juxtaposition of proper names Pythionike Aphrodite, and a temple is more than altars. It is true that Philip's father Amyntas, it seems, had a temple in Amphipolis,[7] but we hear only that this shrine was called ᾽Αμύντειον, nothing, however, of a connection with an Olympian god. The following difference is even more important: the few examples that exist of the cult of living persons or of those who have just died in the period before 326 B.C.—from the honoring of Lysander in Samos (probably in 404 B.C.)[8] to the cults which

---

[5] Cf. Eitrem, *RE.,* see under "Heros," 1123, 48 ff.: 1130, 8 ff.

[6] Cf. Chr. Habicht, *"Gottmenschentum und griechische Städte," Zetemata,* 14, 1956, 14 with n. 2.

[7] Cf. Habicht p. 11.

[8] Habicht, p. 3. About the statues of Lysander and of his nauarchs that the Lacedaemonians erected in Delphi between the statues of gods in 404 B.C., cf. J. Pouilloux-G. Roux, *Énigmes à Delphes,* 1963, 16 ff. Cf. *ibid,* pp. 69 ff. about the treas-

Alexander perhaps already at that time, that is, while still living, came across in Greek cities in Asia Minor[9]—show that a city granted such honors to a liberator or deliverer.[10] Here, however, it is not a city but an individual who originates the cult and not for a "benefactor of the state," but for a very private benefactor.[11] The absurdity of it becomes clear when one asks whom she benefited and whereof the benefit consisted!

The manner in which Harpalos honored Pythionike was therefore in every way scandalous: the honor was greater, and the donor and especially the recipient were less than had hitherto been the custom.

Needless to say, the Pythionike cult has none of the power to form a community which is normally characteristic of the hero cult whether it concerns a genuine or fictitious ancestor or a man or group of men who have done extraordinary services for their city or state. As far as Harpalos is concerned, personal attachment to his mistress is apparently all that he needs to start a cult for her. And it remains obscure how far genuine feeling beside vanity, how far religious ideas and political considerations had a say in his case. Nothing serious will have been at stake, we may be sure.

While he was planning to found a cult to his dead mistress, old myths and Oriental fairy tales seem to have gone to his head, for instance the story that Agamemnon had erected a temple to Aphrodite Argynnos on the Cephissus in Boeotia, in memory of his favorite Argynnos who was drowned there (Phanokles fr. 5, Clem. Al., *Protr.* 32); or the story of the

---

ury of Brasidas. Isocrates in his praise of the dead Evagoras (*ca.* 365 B.C.) claims (§ 8) that he writes the first encomion in prose and says (§ 72): ὥστ' εἴ τινες τῶν ποιητῶν περί τινος τῶν γεγενημένων ὑπερβολαῖς κέχρηνται, λέγοντες ὡς ἦν θεὸς ἐν ἀνθρώποις ἢ δαίμων θνητός, ἅπαντα τὰ τοιαῦτα περὶ τὴν ἐκείνου φύσιν ῥηθῆναι μάλιστ' ἂν ἁρμόσειεν. (Cf. R. Harder, *Eigenart der Griechen*, 1962, 35.) θεὸς ἐν ἀνθρώποις is apparently taken from *Il.* 24, 258, where Priam says about the dead Hector: ὃς θεὸς ἔσκε μετ' ἀνδράσιν.

[9] Habicht, pp. 17–25.

[10] For details see Habicht's thoughtful and thorough treatment.

[11] Similar Aphrodites appear in Demetrios Poliorketes, but Demochares (F Gr Hist. 75 F 1 = Athen., 6, 62, p. 252 F) maintains that Demetrios would have been sad if he had heard that the Athenians had so honoured his hetaira in order to flatter him.

Egyptian Greeks that the smallest pyramid belonged to the *hetaira* Rhodopis (Herodot. 2, 134). This strikes us all as more Oriental than Western and reminds us a little of the Taj Mahal in Agra which the Shah Jehan had built for his favorite wife in the seventeenth century.

More clearly than the honors done the dead Pythionike, it is those granted the living Glykera that show the development of such superhuman honors in Greece and their topical-political importance at the time of Alexander's campaign in India. It is indeed worth discussing them more closely. The honors done Glykera which Theopompus enumerates were likewise unusual for their time. They consisted of two different forms, profane Greek honors such as statues and garlands, and Persian honors normally shown to kings, such as the apostrophe "queen" (which might also be Macedonian, of course) and *proskynesis*. To begin with the latter: that kings are divine is both an Oriental and an early Greek belief. But already in Homer kings are no longer divine even if they are called of divine forbear (διογενεῖς). Their office and their scepter, they have from Zeus; but they are shown only profane honors.[12] In the Eastern monarchies, however, the old ideas have partly survived. And precisely in early Hellenistic times, the old tradition, even though in a new shape, begins to gain ground.

The profane Greek honors (for example, the dedication of statues) had not always been profane but originated in certain religious ideas, particularly in two: first in the idea that a man as "liberator," *soter*, appeared "like a god," and second that a man in a certain elevated situation, which also had its fixed place in public worship, was looked upon as "godlike," at a marriage, for instance, or as the victor in one of the festive contests.[13] When such honors lose all association with these old, strictly defined, and clearly limited cultic and religious functions, they can be combined with the ideas of the "divine

---

[12] It means something different when Priam says of the dead Hector: θεὸς ἔσκε μετ' ἀνδράσιν, cf. above p. 128, n. 8.

[13] On the *makarismos* in such instances, see above, p. 93.

deliverer." Here we can see clearly how the relationship of men to the gods has changed.

Nausikaa saves Odysseus' life, and he promises her, on his departure (*Od.* 8, 467), to direct daily prayers of thanksgiving to her as to a goddess. When, however, some person saves another not only privatim, as an individual, but, for instance, when a state protects a group of people, the liberated can direct their prayers of thanks to the community, indeed hold out a prospect of their sacrifice and alms as though the "Olympian gods" were the deliverers (Aesch., *Suppl.* 980 ff.). In this way an individual can also be glorified as the deliverer of a city and as a ϑεὸς ἐπιφανής, an "appearing god," when one hopes he will bring fortune to the city. So it is, for example, that the first slave (i.e., Demosthenes) in Aristophanes' *Knights* greets the sausage dealer.[14] It is from such ideas that the late-fifth-century custom for a state to bestow cult honors on a human deliverer grows. We have already learned of such ideas which determined the fundamentally Hellenistic ruler cult in the hero worship that Harpalos had transferred to the dead Pythionike.

Theopompus also brings these ideas into play in the honors done the living Glykera; here, too, the distinctions are obliterated; the victor's statue donated for an exceptional success won in cult competition, the statue erected by the community out of gratitude to the deliverer and benefactor, and the religious image dedicated to the hero or the god—into none of these categories can the statues to Glykera be fitted. The only possible precedent could be a statue which Praxiteles had dedicated to the *hetaira* Phryne in Delphi, but this was evidently meant to be a statue of Aphrodite, even if everyone knew that it was Phryne.[15] This affair had caused an uproar

---

[14] 146 ff. . . . ὦ μακάριε . . . ἀνάβαινε σωτὴρ τῇ πόλει. Cf. 458 καὶ τῇ πόλει σωτὴρ φανεὶς ἡμῖν τε τοῖς πολίταις.

[15] Cf. Raubitschek, *RE.*, see under "Phryne." Such things were not necessarily more offensive than in the Madonnas of Fra Filippo Lippi; and Praxiteles was not even a monk whom one could blame for mixing up his divine and his earthly love.

and may well have incited Harpalos to put up statues to his *hetaira.*

And then there is the Persian element, the most alien but politically the most significant factor, the ruler cult, and especially the *proskynesis.* Herodotus had already mentioned it as an Eastern reverence shown to kings (1, 119; 8, 118, etc.), but the Greeks found such kowtowing undignified; at the most they reserved it for the gods.[16] The Oriental king, however, expected it from his subjects—even if precisely the Persians did not identify, or did no longer identify, their king with a god.

The superhuman honors take on therewith a significance completely different from that which the Greeks had ascribed to them before. Habicht has shown in his book[17] that the early Greek ruler cult was no "apotheosis," that is to say, no deification of a human being. The underlying thought was that a human being could reveal divine qualities through some particular deed and thereby win the recognition of the community.

In Glykera's case the statues and garlands with which she is honored are one with the requirement that she be addressed as queen and honored with *proskynesis.* Here then it is a matter of homage to a person, of the claim to show her reverence as though she had become a higher being. It is no wonder that the result is somewhat dubious, when so many heterogeneous themes are brought together, themes which have lost their original significance. The *hetaira* as god queen is simply ridiculous.

Nevertheless there are serious undertones, for the questions arising here touch the roots of the Hellenistic ruler ideology,[18] of the Roman emperor worship, and of the conception of divine

---

[16] Cf., for example, P. Stengel, *Die griechischen Kultusaltertümer,* 3, 1920, 80 f. Habicht (215, 75) quotes Charlesworth's formulation: "the Greeks looked upon prostration not as an ἀσεβές but as an αἰσχρόν."

[17] See especially pp. 172 ff.

[18] On the importance of the "God-Man" in Augustus' time and its connection with Alexander, cf. J. Finck's recent article in *Festschrift Max Wegner,* Münster, 1962, 33 ff. with bibliography. C. J. Classen, *Gymnasium* 70, 1963, 312–338.

grace which held its ground in medieval Europe up to the threshold of our own day. It is the start of one of the most burning and important political problems with which Alexander was faced especially in the years around 326 B.C., and it is this above all that makes *Agen* important.

The god incarnation of the king was for Alexander an extremely important and highly complex problem. Tarn, in his book on Alexander, defines the situation as follows (1, 138): "In Egypt Alexander was an autocrat and a god. In Asia he was an autocrat, but not a god. In old Greece he was a god, but not an autocrat. In Macedonia he was neither autocrat nor god, but a quasi-constitutional king over against whom his people enjoyed certain customary rights."

Whether all this is correct may be open to question, but at all events it was evidently not possible to build up a large uniform state without giving it some form of a religious foundation. The Greek city-state had its cult of the πολιοῦχοι θεοί, of the gods who protected the *polis*, but it could not be adopted by the new kingdom in its entirety, because belief in the gods was already seriously on the wane. A sufficiently powerful profane theory of state, which could have made the power of the king plausible and which assured the allegiance of the various subjects, did not exist either. Both Theopompus and Python demonstrate the danger of the de-Hellenization and barbarization of the new state, and point to an open wound. But the "liberation of Greece" of which Theopompus speaks was not enough to win over loyal non-Greeks. Python's mockery of freedom (which Alexander certainly did not find as disagreeable as Theopompus' ideology) could be taken as an inclination for the Macedonian hereditary monarchy or for Oriental despotism—but these two forms of government were quite different. If the Greeks neither lived any longer according to the old traditions and religious ideas nor in the new philosophical constitution of a Plato or Aristotle, monarchy was the only remaining form of government for a large territorial state. If, however, the sovereign could only win authority and legality through religious consecration, Alexander had not yet fixed on any definite form for it.[19] This, however, soon followed and remained fixed for centuries to follow until in England, the United States, and the France of the Revolution a form of democracy was found with the aid of the representation of the people which could function outside a city-state.[20]

As is well known, these problems caused Alexander his first serious difficulties when, in 327 B.C., a year before the performance of *Agen*, he tried in Bactria to make the Greek participants in a symposium prostrate themselves.[21]

Harpalos does not seem to have demanded that the Greeks prostrate themselves before Glykera, or otherwise Theopompus, who is intent on putting Harpalos' behavior in as scandalous a light as possible, would certainly have mentioned it. He merely says that she was addressed as queen in Tarsos ὑπὸ τοῦ πλήθους (as in F 254a) or ὑπὸ τοῦ λαοῦ (as in F 253), by the multitude and the people, and honored with *proskynesis*, but this is obviously a reference to Orientals.

Nevertheless, Harpalos was here interfering dangerously in things which had to be handled only with the utmost caution and the greatest tact. In fact, in such a precarious political situation, Harpalos' behavior must have been like a bull's in a china shop.

That Theopompus and Python took up these matters was politically significant because Harpalos[22] was no mere nobody,

[19] Wilamowitz, *Glaube der Hellenen*, 2, 264, maintains that Alexander had to introduce the ruler cult. Habicht, however, has shown that Alexander was content—and had to be content—as far as the Greek cities were concerned with being their benefactor and *soter*. From the Persians he naturally expected that they looked upon him as successor to their kings.

[20] How far "representative government" was developed in ancient times is fully discussed by J. A. O. Larsen in his Sather Lectures of 1955: *Representative Government in Greek and Roman History*.

[21] Cf. especially Chares, F Gr Hist. 125 F 14, and Arrian 4, 10, 5 ff. for the echo of the lively discussion on the various forms of divine honours which are also instructive for the honours shown Pythionike and Glykera, and 11, 8 ff. for the discussion of *proskynesis*. Clem. Alex., *Protr.* 4, 54, states that the Athenians had already done Philip *proskynesis*; but cf. Nilsson, *Gr. Rel.*, 2, 134, 6.

[22] E. Badian, *JHSt.* 81, 1961, 16–43—the latest on him.

but Alexander's right-hand man, assigned to govern the kingdom. He was born of a Macedonian princely family, was related to the royal house by marriage, and a friend of Alexander's since youth: when the nineteen-year-old crown prince had to flee the court with his mother Olympias, Harpalos went to Illyria with them. As Harpalos was not suited to military service, Alexander used him in civil and financial administration.

Once before, after the battle of Issus, Harpalos had had to run away because he was afraid of being punished. But Alexander had forgiven him and appointed him chief administration officer in Tarsos and Babylon. There, he disposed of the royal treasury and squandered money, we hear, not only on women but also on tasty fishes and the like. Since he supplied Alexander with books on his journey eastward (Plut., *Alex.* 8), he was evidently not uncultured. Momentary impulses rather than careful and responsible planning were characteristic of him. Later, chiefly in Athens, he revealed himself to be a *type débrouillard* rather than a serious politician.

Although Theopompus and Python warned Alexander about Harpalos, he remained faithful to him. After Alexander's return, when Harpalos fled for the second time, and with the royal treasury into the bargain, Alexander's first reaction was to have the messengers who brought him the news arrested as informers (Plut., *Alex.* 41). Like many other flippant characters of history, Harpalos must have had personal charm. Evidently Alexander was not quite so good at choosing high civil servants as he was at choosing generals—and probably had less suitable people for civil duties at his disposal: the Macedonians had little practice in such things, and the Iranians were disloyal wherever possible. At all events, in 324 B.C. Alexander felt obliged to carry out such a purge among his satraps that it nearly came to a catastrophe.

It is impossible for us now to tell what Harpalos' idea was in having his mistresses and himself shown such honors. Theopompus, who likens them to the honors due Alexander and his family, evidently interprets it as political usurpation. Perhaps, however, Harpalos was merely a half-Hellenized Macedonian who suddenly saw himself promoted into the splendor and enchantment of Greek culture and Oriental power without any sense of the duties which suddenly fell to the Macedonians. (How aristocratic the Attic democrats of the fifth century seem in comparison, though they, too, had their occasional lapses!)

Those Macedonians who did not happen to have the good fortune to be educated by Aristotle were more easily liable to such corruption and the somewhat childlike, not to say childish, hankering after a "grand life." In the history of the world, this situation has caused mischief time and time again, but with particularly disastrous results in Alexander's kingdom, for the new state was not strong on its feet, and the world-historic task of making Greek culture a world culture was a big one. It was a bad sign if a *bonvivant* with his mistresses could presume to usurp the divine humanity of a king, the one thing capable of keeping the state together.

There may not have been any definite political aims behind Glykera's receiving such honors. If the dead Pythionike had become Aphrodite, Harpalos and his mistress probably did not find it unreasonable that her successor should be given at least royal honors. That it had disastrous political results he may not have noticed; indeed, even Alexander may not have realized it. At all events, he neglected Theopompus' and Python's warnings.

There is scarcely any doubt that *Agen* was performed in public. In that case the soldiers must have listened to it as well, those same soldiers who shortly before had refused—or were about to refuse—to take any further part in adventures eastward, who had left no one in any doubt about their desire to return home, and who had forced Alexander to give up all his further plans.

Many a Macedonian may have felt distressed during the performance of this merry play which vividly portrayed the dissolute life of a man in a responsible position and the orientalization of the state hierarchy. And Alexander, when he saw himself appear at the end to put everything to rights, could not ignore the summons to return home at once and take measures against his closest friends.

Whether the play was performed (and this sounds probable) when Alexander had already made up his mind to forego all further plans and return home, or shortly before, one thing is remarkable—that such freedom of speech, παρρησία, was possible in his camp. But it is not beyond the bounds of possibility that Alexander looked upon such things with generous amusement.

There was some kind of literary life in Alexander's retinue, for we hear from various sources that poets and philosophers (scientists as well) accompanied him. Later commentators looked upon the poets, it is true, as flatterers.[23] That they were not there merely in order to flatter, but that Alexander's closest circle was also culturally well-versed is shown by the one fact that a quotation from Euripides was enough to cost Kleitos his head.[24] (The Sophocles quotations in *Agen* point in much the same direction.)

Considering how little of the play is extant, it is precarious to say too much about Python's satyr drama. But the impression we had from our examination of the metrical forms seems to me to be corroborated. That the lines of the play are not simply offered us "without obligation" is proof of the quality of the play. When one takes the text seriously, it yields references in several directions, and a meaningful whole, even if only in vague outlines, becomes visible.

---

[23] Plut., *De Alex.* fort. 9, 331 A ποιηταὶ κολακεύοντες αὐτοῦ τὴν τύχην. *id. quom. adul.* 24, 65 C ἦν δ' ὁ Μήδειος τοῦ περὶ 'Αλέξανδρον χοροῦ τῶν κολάκων οἷος ἔξαρχος. Curt. 8, 5, 8 mentions Agis of Argos and Cleon from Sicily *et cetera urbium suarum purgamenta* as *perniciosa adulatio.* For these poets see Tarn, 2, 55 ff. How far it was flattery that led Python to make Alexander appear at the end of the play, we cannot judge—before, he had, exactly like Theopompus, said many things which cannot have been exactly to Alexander's taste, which, by the way, refutes the surmise voiced also in antiquity that Alexander could have written the play himself.

[24] *Androm.* 683 οἴμοι καθ' 'Ελλάδ' ὡς κακῶς νομίζεται, "Alas, how badly things stand in Greece." Cf. Plut., *Alex.* 51.

Nowadays it is customary to sneer at the dramatic form as a mixture of satyr drama and Attic comedy.[25] It is true that *Agen,* unlike the other satyr dramas of the fifth century we know but like the old Attic comedy, handles a topical, political theme and includes the appearance of contemporary figures. Serious tragedy did not restrict itself to mythical characters: not only early times had brought topical political themes onto the stage (in Phrynichus' *Capture of Miletus* and *Phoenician Women* or Aeschylus' *Persians,* for example), but also later writers like Theodektes, Moschion, and no doubt the author of *Gyges* had had resort to historical subjects. In addition, in Python's time the comedy had ceased to say a word to its time, and we should be grateful to him for not missing the chance of staging so splendid a scene as the conjuring up of Pythionike by Satyrs dressed up as *magi.* This and all else we know of the play is effective theater, tasteful and cultured.

But the most significant thing about the play is this: for the last time, perhaps more even than in Aristophanes who does not dramatize contemporary politics until the great period of the Athenian state is on the decline—perhaps, therefore, for the first time since Aeschylus' *Persians,* a breath of world history blows across the Greek stage—even if it is a Greek stage erected in the Far East. And here once again the tension between Greece and Persia, between West and East, is the subject. But whereas the Persian wars of the fifth century, as Aeschylus clearly and validly brought out in his play, helped a new man, a pioneer, to victory, the foundations of Alexander's kingdom remained unstable and problematical.

In his satyr drama Python aims straight at what in later history repeatedly compromised the dignity of a king (as was the case with the *diadochi,* the Roman emperors, and the medieval princes who lived by the grace of God)—namely the usurpation of this grace by a charlatan. Python brings out splendidly the absurdity and the uncanniness of such *hubris* as we see it in Harpalos by making the Satyrs dressed up as

[25] Suess, *De Graecorum fabulis satyricis,* Dorpat, 1924, 7 ff.—often repeated since.

Persian necromancers conjure up the *hetaira* who has been proclaimed a goddess.

Python takes up the old theme which we have pursued through several dramas, the relationship of man to the gods, in a new, burlesque form, but it is all underlined, if I am not mistaken, by the poet's own serious concern.

Surely, Python's *Agen* deserves to be better known.

Appendix

The Florence Papyrus
of Aeschylus' *Myrmidons*

THE FULL TEXT of this important papyrus is pre-
sented here for two reasons: First, the verses 1–14 may help the reader
of my translation (above, p. 3), and so I have given here more
supplements than otherwise would have been justified. Second, I
hope to give some new readings. I am presenting an *apparatus criticus*
enumerating the most important supplements proposed by other
scholars and a description of the dubious letters as they appeared to
me from my own collation of the manuscript. I have to thank Miss
Teresa Lodi—who at that time was director of the Biblioteca
Laurenziana—for allowing me, ten years ago, to study this text.

I have taken special care in defining the exact length of the gaps
in the beginnings of the lines, by drawings on transparent paper, and
I always tried to copy the groups of letters proposed for the supplements from other parts of the papyrus, where such groups occur.[1]

---

[1] In other papyri too, editors occasionally do not take sufficient regard of the length
of the beginnings of lines. K. Reinhardt, for instance (*Hermes*, 85, 1957, 7), supposes
that in the papyrus of Aeschylus' *Isthmiastai* (fr. 17 M.) verses 39–46 are not trimeters
but tetrameters. But the ἔκθεσις of the tetrameters would be much too large; there
would be 8–9 letters to the left of the beginnings of the trimeters, whereas the tetrameters of verses 18–22 have only 3–4 letters more to the left than the trimeters verses
23 ff. In fact, the difficulties Reinhardt sees are no reason to abandon the trimeters:
that line 46 begins too far to the right is a mere printer's error in my edition (which I
am sorry to have overlooked), and for the supplements of the sentence in verses 43 ff.
there is room in line 42—although I do not risk making any proposals. Besides, in
verses 41–46 the first letters of the words that begin the trimeters stand so exactly
beneath one another that it cannot be mere chance.

BIBLIOGRAPHY FOR THE PAPYRUS

Norsa, M. and G. Vitelli, *Mélanges Bidez* (1933–1934), II, 968 ff., 1st ed. ———·*Pap. Soc. It.* (1935), XI, 1211.

Fritsch, C. E. "Neue Fragmente des Aischylos und Sophokles" (1936). Doctoral dissertation, Hamburg.

Schadewaldt, W. *Hellas und Hesperien*, pp. 166 ff. = *Hermes* 71 (1936), 25 ff.

Page, D. L. *Select Papyri* (1942), III, 136 (Loeb).

Lloyd-Jones, H. *Aeschylus* (1957), II, 590 (Loeb).

Mette, H. J. *Die Fragmente der Tragödien des Aischylos* (1959), fr. 225.

The Papyrus

λεύ[[σ]]σουσι τοὐμὸν σῶμα; μὴ δόκει ποτέ
πέτρ[ο]ις καταξανϑέντα Πηλέως γόνον
μάχ]ην [π]αρήσειν Τρωϊκὴν ἀνὰ χϑόνα
ὀν]ημένοισι Τρωσὶ τὴν ἄ[ν]ευ δορ[ό]s.

5 ANT.? ἢ το]ι̣ γένοιτ' ἄν, εὐπετεστέρα̣ν δ' ἔχοι̣ς
πρὸς] τοῦτο δή, βροτοῖσιν ἰατρὸν πόνων.

AX. τάρβε]ι̣ δ' Ἀχαιῶν χεῖρ' ἐφορμήσω δορί
χαλ]ῶσαν ὀργῆι ποιμένος κακοῦ διαί;
ἄγ' εἴ]περ εἷς ὤν, ὡς λέγουσι σύμμαχοι,

10 ἧσσα]ν τοσαύτην ἔκτισ' οὐ παρὼν μάχηι,
κείροι]μ' ἐγὼ τὰ πάντ' Ἀχαϊκῶι στρατῶι.
τοῖον] δ' ἀφεῖναι τοῦπος οὐκ αἰδώς μ' ἔχει·
τίς γὰρ] τοιούτ[ο]υ̣ς εὐγενεστέρους ἐμοῦ
ἄρχους ἄ]ν [εἴ]ποι καὶ στρατοῦ ταγ[ε]ύματα;

15 . . . .]. .[..]. . ὑμᾶς εἷς ἀ̣νὴρ ἠ[ι̣]κίζετο
. . . . . .]ταράσσων καὶ πολυσκεδεῖς συ̣ϑείς
. . . .]α̣ τεύχ[η π]ερὶ νέοις βραχ[ίο]σιν
. . . . . .].ευτ[. ..].ϱε⸌⸍πανϑιμων στρατόν
]. . .[..]ων εὐμαρῶς ἐτρ[έ]ψατο̣

20]..[α]ν̣δρο̣ς προδοσίαν ἔγε[ι̣]μ' ἐμοί
ἄ]ν̣δρα τόνδ' αἰ̣σχ[ρῶς] ϑανεῖν
].π̣ᾱ[. . . . .]ρ[..]ν
]οισε[..].ι̣δου̣σι̣ν .. ϱστ[.]μ.ν
]σι κάφανῆ στρα̣τη[λάτην

25]τονδ' ἀπόλλυσι̣ σ̣[τ]ρ̣α̣[τ]ό̣ν
]α̣ς εἶπον οὐ̣ ψευδ[ῆ λ]έγων
]ον τόνδ' ἀποφϑερεῖ στρατόν
μ]ῆνις, ὡς ὁρᾶν πάρα.
δέδ]οικα τὴν ἡγουμένην

30 ἐμ]φανῶς κατήγορος
].. ἐλε[ύ]ϑερον λέγεις
]. . . εὐτυχεστερα
]. α .. ο̣ὐ̣δεὶς φρονεῖ
ο]ὐδαμῶς πρέπει τόδε

35].. αι διαλ[λα]γαί
τ]υχω μειλί[γ]ματι

1 de Λ vix dubitandum |ĊC|MA·|ΔΌΚ|| **2** Π pot. qu. ·]Γ vel Τ|ΘΈΝ||
3]ΗΝ[vestigia incerta |]ΑΡΗ pot. qu.]ΝΗ propter spatium inter
P et Η|μάχην παρήσειν Fritsch, τροπὴν vel μάχην (ἄτην Schwartz,
Pfeiffer brevius, φθορὰν Schad.) ἀνήσειν N.-V., Δανάους ὀνήσειν Page
|ΩΪ|| **4** ὄν] Fr.; καθ]ημένοισι N.-V., Körte sine dubio longius spatio;
ἀλλ᾽] ἠμένοισι Page | Ά, suppl. N.-V. || **5**]Ι pot. qu.]Ρ (cave ne
decipiaris vestigiis atrimenti obliti), suppl. Sn.; οὐ γὰ]ρ N.-V., longius;
καίτο]ι Fr., longius | PAN, vix PON | δ᾽ ἔχοις N.-V., quamquam Λ vel
Χ pot. qu. Δ|ΟΙC vel ΟΥC || **5** sq. Achillis interlocutori dederunt
N.-V., i.e., Antilocho? (Sulzberger) || **6** suppl. N.-V.; τὸν] P. Maas,
brevius |ῙΑ| ΩΝ·|| **7** φόβω]ι Schad., sed longius spatio, itaque τάρβε]ι
N.-V.; δέε]ι?|ΧΕῖΡΑ|| **8** suppl. Fr.; μαιμ]ῶσαν N.-V., longius | fin. v.
7 adscr. ἀν(τὶ) ἕνεκα|| **9** ἀλλ᾽ εἴ] vel κἄν, εἴ] N.-V., longiora; ἄγ᾽ εἴ] Sn.
|ΈΙC|| **10** τροπὴ]ν N.-V., Schad., longius; βλάβη]ν Pfeiffer, Eitrem;
ἧσσα]ν Sn., fort. paullo brevius; ἄτη]ν Schwartz, Pfeiffer, brevius
|ΈΚΤΙC᾽|| **11** σώσαι]μ᾽ N.-V.; [ὅδ᾽ εἴ]μ᾽ Körte, brevius; [ὅδε εἴ]μ᾽ Schad.,
sed scriptio plena non invenitur nisi v. 7 χεῖρα; ὧδ᾽ εἴ]μ᾽ N.-V.²;
πορθοῖ]μ᾽ Fr., fort. longius; κείροι]μ᾽ Sn. |ΕΤΩΙ:ΕΓΩ Πᵖᶜ|ΝΤ᾽|ΑΧΑΙΚΩΙ:
Πᵖᶜ|| **12**]Δ᾽ pot. qu.]Τ᾽ |τοῖον] N.-V., τορῶς Mette |ΤΟῨΠ|Μ᾽ add.
Πᵖᶜ|ΕΚΕΙ: N.-V. || **13** καὶ γάρ] N.-V., τίς γὰρ] Fr. | cet. N.-V. || **14**
οὐδεὶς ἄ]ν N.-V.; ἀγοὺς Körte, brevius; ἄρχους Fr. |]Π,]Ι sim., suppl.
N.-V. |ΤΑΓ[.]Υ, vix ΤΑΡ[.]Γ, suppl. N.-V. || **15**]CΜ[?, fort. Κύκνο]ς
(Schad.)?|πάντα]ς μ[άλ]ᾳ [[η]] ὑμᾶς? (δ'ὅτε Schad. vestig. non conv.) || **16**
φευκτοὺς] Schad., longius; δειλοὺς]?|]ΤΑ vel]ΓΑ|ΕῙC|ϹΙΘΕΙC:ϹΥΘΕΙC
Πᵖᶜ? συθείς Vit., Schad.; τιθείς Sulzberger, Kalén, quod equidem
legere non possum || **17**]Α,]Λ|Χ[pot. qu. Λ[; λαβὼν τ]ὰ Schad., i.e.,
Cycnus, sed aptius ad Achillem referendum esse vid., itaque temptes
τίς θεὶς τ]ὰ τεύχη――[ἔσωσεν] εὖ π[ως τό]νδε πένθιμον στρατόν, [πλῆθος]
δὲ Τ[ρώ]ων vel δύσας τ]ὰ τεύχη――[τίς δὴ τότ'] εὖ γ᾽ [ἐπε]ῖδε κτλ.|ΑΧ[,
ΑΛ[|]C pot. qu.]Ε|| **18**]Κ,]Τ,]Γ,]C sim. | de E vix dubitandum
|Π[, Τ[, Ν[| fort.]ΟΝΔΕ,]ΕΙΔΕ,]ΕΙΛΕ?|ΠΆΝΘΙΜΟΝ: ΠΑΝΘΊΜΩΝ
Πᵖᶜ, πενθίμων N.-V. | τίς ἀντ᾽ ἐμ]οῦ γ᾽ [ἔσω]σε (quod legi non potest)
πάνθ᾽ ὑμῶν στρατόν Schad. || **19**]Δ,]Ζ,]Ξ|Ο, Ε, sim. |Ι[, Τ[, sim.
]δὲ Τ[ρώ]ων Schad., quod vestigiis optime convenit | fin. suppl.
N.-V. || **20** νῦν δ᾽ ὤν] ἄν[α]νδρος e.g. Sn., vel, cum]ΥΠ[,]ΙΤ[sim.
legendum esse vid., λ]ιπ[α]νδρος? |]Μ pot. qu.]Ν, cetera
incerta, suppl. Sn. || **21** Suppl. N.-V. | init. e.g. κεῖνος, θέλει γ]ὰ[ρ
Sn. || **22**]ΙΠῩ[,]ΙΠΤῩ[sim. |]Ρ[vel]Β[,]ρ[ιο]ν vel]β[ιο]ν?|| **23**

ἐ[ν]διδοῦσι{ν} νόστ[ι]μον?‖ **24**]CI pot. qu.]OI?|ΦΑ pot. qu. ΓΕ, κάγενῆ
Sulzberger, κάφ. Sn. |Α, Λ, Δ|ΤΗ, ΖΙ, ΠΝ sim. |[λατον Sulzb., [λάτην
Sn. ‖ **25** fin. Sn. ‖ **25** sqq. temptes [ὅσπερ πάλαι μὲν] τόνδ' ἀπόλλυσι
στρατόν, [ὅς θ', ὡς πρὸς ὑμ]ᾶς εἶπον οὐ ψευδῆ λέγων [ἄρδην 'Αχαι]ὸν κτλ.‖
26 Ν.-V. ‖ **28** Suppl. N.-V. | temptes: ΑΝΤΙΛ. ἔχει σε δεινῇ‖ **29**]OI, vix
]Ν (Ν.-V.) | ΤΗΝΗΓ vel ΤΗΝΠΡ? (Τ . . ΑΡΝ Ν.-V.) |ἄτην δ' ἐπεὶ
δέδ]οικα, e.g., Sn. ‖ **30** Suppl. N.-V. |σοὶ νῦν ἐπῆλθον?‖ **31** Suppl.
Ν.-V. | ΑΧΙΛΛ.· ἄγαν λόγον σὺ τό]νδ', e.g., Sn. ‖ **32** ΑΝΤΙΛ. φρονῶν τις
ηὗρε πράγματ' εὐτυχέστερα vel sim.? |]ΜΑ[ΤΑ]? ‖ **33** fort. ΑCΜ
| expectes αἰνῶν ὕβριν sim ‖ **34** ἐχθροῖς ἀρήγειν? **36** δυστ]υχῶ Schad.

INDEX

Accius, *Achilles* fr. 1: 6 n. 12
Aeschylus, *Ag.* 613: 9
————. ————. 855: 9f.
————. ————. 1380: 10
————. ————. 1417, 1432: 31
————. ————. 1440: 31
————. *Isthmiast.* 35, 97
————. ————. fr. 17, 39–46: 139 n. 1
————. *Prom.* 266: 11
————. *Septem* 196 ff.: 5
————. ————. 683 ff.: 17
————. fr. 221: 6
————. fr. 225: 3 ff., 139 ff.
————. fr. 227: 16
————. fr. 228 f.: 15
————. fr. 231: 16
αἰδώς: 8 ff.
Alcman fr. 26 P.: 36
ἀμηχανία: 33 f.
Anacreon fr. 417 P.: 43
Ἄορνος: 105 f.
Apollod. 3, 5, 5: 72
Archilochus fr. 6 D.: 8 n. 18
————. fr. 7 D.: 52 f.
————. fr. 79 D.: 12
Aristoph. *Clouds*: 67
————. *Frogs.* 457 ff.: 95 f.
Atalante: 36 f.
Auct. ad Herenn.: 2, 27. 43: 82

Baudelaire: 65
Bellerophon: 35 46

Chaucer, *Canterb: Tales* 2307: 37

δίκη: 11 f., 33

Empedocles fr. 6: 69 n. 27
Euripides: 23–98
————. *Alc.:* 35
————. ————. 939 ff.: 48

————. *Antiope:* 70 ff.
————. ————. fr. 179: 71 f.
————. ————. fr. 181: 71 n. 3
————. ————. fr. 183: 84 f., 92, 95
————. ————. fr. 184: 82, 90
————. ————. fr. 185: 95
————. ————. fr. 186: 83 f., 95
————. ————. fr. 187: 83, 87
————. ————. fr. 188: 86, 92, 97
————. ————. fr. 190: 73
————. ————. fr. 193: 88, 90
————. ————. fr. 194: 88, 90
————. ————. fr. 196: 88, 95
————. ————. fr. 198: 87, 90, 95
————. ————. fr. 199: 88
————. ————. fr. 200: 88 f.
————. ————. fr. 203: 77 n. 17
————. ————. fr. 204: 74
————. ————. fr. 205: 76, 80
————. ————. fr. 206: 74 n. 11
————. ————. fr. 208: 76, 80, 88 n. 39
————. ————. fr. 209: 78 n. 19
————. ————. fr. 210: 74 n. 11
————. ————. fr. 211: 76
————. ————. fr. 213: 77 n. 19
————. ————. fr. 216: 74 n. 12, 75
————. ————. fr. 218: 75
————. ————. fr. 219: 86 n. 34
————. ————. fr. 220: 64 f.
————. ————. fr. 910: 90 f.
————. ————. fr. 1023: 82
————. *Belleroph.* fr. 297: 61, 65
————. *Chrysippus* fr. 840 f.: 63 f.
————. *Hipp. I* fr. 430: 26, 39 f., 51
————. ————. fr. 431: 38
————. ————. fr. 433: 38
————. ————. fr. 443: 27
————. ————. fr. 444: 29 f., 61
————. ————. p. 491, N²: 28 n. 6, 30
————. *Hipp. II* 13 ff.: 68 f.
————. ————. 47: 29

Index